THE AMERICAN NEGRO

HIS HISTORY AND LITERATURE

PROCEEDINGS

OF THE

NATIONAL NEGRO CONFERENCE
1909

ARNO PRESS and THE NEW YORK TIMES
NEW YORK 1969

General Editor
WILLIAM LOREN KATZ

THIS BOOK RECORDS THE FIRST STEPS IN THE founding of the NAACP, one of the most important events in the struggle for black equality in the ninety years between Reconstruction and the beginning of the sit-ins. Like the civil rights movements of the last half of the 1860's and the first half of the 1960's, the NAACP was an interracial crusade for legal and political justice. White liberals played key roles in the establishment of the NAACP and for the next decade provided most of its leadership. Sixteen of the speeches in this volume are by whites, eight by blacks, a fair index of the relative weight of the two races in the Association's early years.

The NAACP was the product of two major developments in the first decade of the twentieth century: 1) the deteriorating civil and political status of the Negro coupled with an alarming increase in anti-Negro violence; 2) a reaction by black militants and white liberals against the gospel of accommodation and gradualism preached by Booker T. Washington. From 1898 to 1908 at least 934 Negroes were lynched, many with unspeakable brutality. During the same decade there were several race riots in southern and northern cities that took an appalling toll of black lives. Between 1890 and 1908 every southern state disfranchised all its black voters by means of poll taxes, white primaries, and literacy or property qualification tests enforced against Negroes but not against whites. These years also witnessed the passage of a host of Jim Crow laws that segregated the Negro in every aspect of Southern life. The beginnings of Harlem, South Side Chicago, and other black ghettoes also date from the early years of the century.

In the face of this worsening situation, Booker T. Washington's strategy of temporary accommodation to white supremacy while the Negro pulled himself upward by the acquisition of property, trades, and education (especially vocational training), seemed increasingly obsolete to a growing number of black militants. In 1905 a group of predominantly northern, college-trained black men, led by W. E. B. DuBois, organized the Niagara Movement to demand full equality *now*. Racially exclusive (whites were not admitted to full membership), the Niagara Movement lacked the power, money, and influence to achieve a major impact, and by 1909 it was moribund. Meanwhile a handful of white liberals, some of abolitionist descent, began discussing the need to revive the abolitionist commitment to racial equality. "It is time for the colored people to organize for lawful self-defense and for white lovers of liberty to stand up for equal rights," declared William Lloyd Garrison, Jr., in 1906.

Three years later Oswald Garrison Villard, prominent New York journalist and grandson of *The Liberator's* editor, expressed his disillusionment with Booker T. Washington: "I grow very weary of hearing it said that Hampton and Tuskegee provide the absolute solution to this problem." With Washington, "it is always the same thing, platitudes, stories, high praise for the Southern white man who is helping the negro up, insistence that the way to favor lies through owning lands and farms, etc." In 1908, after a vicious race riot at Springfield, Illinois, a group of concerned whites and blacks began meeting at the New York apartment of William English Walling (a socialist journalist) to discuss the founding of a Negro rights association. The group, of Anglo-Saxon, Negro, and Jewish ancestry and including social workers, socialists, journalists, clergymen, and descendants of abolitionists, decided to issue a call for a national conference on the race problem. The call, written by Villard and published on the centenary of Lincoln's birth, proclaimed that " 'A house divided against itself cannot stand'; this government cannot exist half-slave and half-free any better today than it could in 1861. . . . [There must be] a renewal of the struggle for civil and political liberty."

The speeches, discussions, and resolutions passed at the 1909 Conference are preserved in this volume. It is an important historical document, for the Conference foreshadowed the future course of the

NAACP. The problem of lynching, the denial of civil and political rights, inferior educational facilities for black people, the racist doctrine of Negro inferiority, the need for a national association to fight for equal justice in the courts, the press, and Congress—all of these issues were discussed by the 1909 Conference. The resolutions denounced "the ever-growing oppression of our 10,000,000 colored fellow citizens . . . the systematic persecution of law-abiding citizens and their disfranchisement on account of their race alone," and demanded enforcement of the 14th and 15th Amendments. The second annual Conference was held in 1910, at which the official name of The National Association for the Advancement of Colored People was adopted and permanent organizational machinery established. The origin of the NAACP, however, dates from the 1909 Conference, whose *Proceedings* are still exciting and relevant reading today.

James M. McPherson
DEPARTMENT OF HISTORY
PRINCETON UNIVERSITY

Proceedings of the
National Negro Conference
1909

New York
May 31 and June 1

CONTENTS

PREFACE

Early in 1909 some twenty persons met together in New York City for the purpose of utilizing the public interest in the Lincoln Centennial in behalf of our colored fellow citizens. Within a few weeks this number was enlarged to about fifty, one-third of whom were from other cities than New York. From the outset this committee was composed of white and colored people alike, and represented the most varied opinions; all agreed only in the feeling that no one of the great efforts now being made by the Negroes or by whites in their behalf or all of them put together fully responded to the needs of the situation.

It was the opinion of all the members of the preliminary committee,* and I believe also of every one of those since interested in the Conference, that the most neglected side of the Negro's welfare is his right to civil and political equality, recognized for nearly half a century in this country and clearly expressed in the Constitution.

It was realized that no organization then existed, composed of colored and white people alike, that was making its main object the preservation of these rights, now threatened from so many quarters. It was considered highly important to establish a re-

---

*The Committee invites communications of all kinds, not only questions as to its work, but all possible information and suggestions concerning the civil and political status of the colored people and related matters, the deteriorating effects of civil and political wrongs on general welfare; and also with reference to the indirect effect of such civil and political disabilities on those white elements of the population which, being most similarly situated to the Negroes in their daily life and occupations, are often similarly affected by the prevailing persecution.

lation between organizations already in existence as well as among individuals who, while working for the colored population primarily in some other direction, were also firmly decided to stand for the Negro's political and civil rights, but were unable to do so effectively on account of the absence of such an established relationship.

The same unanimity that prevailed in regard to the main objects of the new organization extended also to its choice of methods. It was decided that a series of conferences would be the best means at once to attract the attention of all those who might become interested in the proposed organization, to put the present situation of the Negro in its entirety in the foreground of public interest and to establish a basis of fact, reasoned policy and even of science for its future conduct.

The first Conference was necessarily of a general character. It is hoped and believed that each of the coming conferences will be limited to a more definite field, and therefore give results of a still greater scientific value. The intention is, also, to make them even more thoroughly representative of the whole body of opinion in this country that stands for *all* the rights of the colored population including equal opportunity to enter into and to rise in every field of employment, public and private, *without exception.*

The results of the first Conference more than justified the greatest hopes of its promoters. The programme, as arranged, while covering a very broad field, showed the feasibility of building up an organization on these lines. The character of the delegations composing the Conference and its final action proved the possibility of securing harmony between half a dozen different currents of opinion favoring the Negroes, already existing among the white population, and a similar number of diverging movements among the colored people themselves.

It is confidently believed that the proceedings of the first Conference of 1909 and the resolutions passed will serve as a convincing appeal for public support, that they will bring not only a very large increase in the number of those attending the conference but also new forces which will strengthen it for the work it has already undertaken, broaden its scope and define still more clearly the friendly attitude of all public-spirited and democratic citizens.

In view of the resolutions adopted in 1909 it is scarcely necessary to state that it is the deep conviction of all that not only the ultimate solution of the problem but the crying necessities of the moment will be best met *not by any suppression or postponement* of the fullest and freest possible discussion of the question in all its aspects, but *by bringing it into the very foreground of public attention.* Every available means should be adopted for this purpose, not only investigations of the situation in all of its manifold forms and in every section of the country, but also conferences, public meetings, speeches and articles by members of the organization and all others interested, co-operation with other organizations and the furnishing to the public press of news hitherto suppressed or difficult to obtain.

By all these and other means it is hoped and believed that the so-called Negro question, in its broader aspects, will become more and more a subject of daily interest to all classes of the American people, until the nation is at last in a mood to deal with this momentous evil of race discrimination in the thoroughgoing spirit with which alone it can be successfully handled.

W. E. W.

NATIONAL NEGRO CONFERENCE HEADQUARTERS,
500 FIFTH AVENUE,
NEW YORK CITY.

Address of

William Hayes Ward

Editor The Independent

New York

The purpose of this conference is to emphasize in word
and, so far as possible, in act, the principle that equal justice should be done to man as man, and particularly to the
Negro, without regard to race, color or previous condition of servitude.   It is not strange that with the abolition of slavery, and the legal and nominal grant of suffrage and equal rights to care for himself, there should
have followed, with many among us, a cooling sympathy,
or the thought that our duty was all done and that now
the freedman could look out for himself as the rest of
us do.   As the years have passed and a new generation
has come which has no memory of the Civil War or of
the Proclamation of Emancipation, and no knowledge of
the efforts made during the period of reconstruction and
the adoption of the Fourteenth and Fifteenth Amendments to reduce the Negro back to a condition of serfdom, we need not wonder that the old fervor of sympathy has much subsided, while at the same time there has
been a readiness to apologize for old wrongs; and we
have even seen the effort, too often successful, to pervert
the history of the old struggle.

There is an absolute divergence of view between the
ruling majority in the South, who desire to hold the

Negro in virtual serfdom, and ourselves. They are, in a degree, honest in their position, if not Christian. They believe that the Negro is essentially inferior, something less than fully human, half a brute, and incapable of reaching the standard of civilization. This is an ignorant position, but yet actually held and believed. I suppose that it is not generally known what is the scientific basis of that popular opinion which still finds its expression in speeches, editorials, and books, and even in popular novels and plays. For that belief the responsibility rests on a book which for some years before the Civil War had great circulation and influence, and which was the armory from which the defenders of slavery drew their weapons and ammunition. It was entitled "The Types of Mankind" by Nott and Glidden. Dr. Nott was a physician and he contributed to the work all the data of anatomy and ethnology which could be gathered to show the physical and mental inferiority of the Negro. Particularly he argued that the smaller brain and simpler brain structure of the Negro made it absolutely impossible that he could ever rise to be anything more than an inferior and subject race. Mr. Glidden had been a traveler in Egypt, somewhat of a student of its antiquities, and he contributed the evidence that in the time of the Egyptian grandeur the Negro was also subject and slave; and to this he added all the proofs possible to show the degraded condition of the various Negro tribes, their cannibalism and sensuality, their resistance to civilization, and the conclusion that to them slavery has been the greatest blessing. The book had a great vogue. It claimed to give the last word of science. Its conclusions were very pleasing to those who profited by slavery, and to this day, while the book is forgotten, its assertions are repeated as if they were still uncontradicted, and a multitude of people believe them true.

Doubtless Dr. Nott believed them true. Immediately

after the Civil War he had occasion to reiterate them with intense and personal emphasis. He was at the head of a medical school in Mobile, Alabama. The school was broken up, and the premises vacated. General O. O. Howard, at the head of the Freedmen's Bureau, seized the building for a school for Negroes. It was actually an attempt to disprove the assertions which Dr. Nott had made of Negro incapacity. Dr. Nott was most indignant and utterly outraged. He wrote a pamphlet in protest, a copy of which I have in my hands, in which he not only bitterly assailed our government for seizing the premises, but with all the fury of an old prophet he foretold the sure failure of emancipation. He declared that the Negro could not support himself, that he would starve to death, unless the country, that is, the North, which had emancipated him, should feed and clothe him as a pauper. Let me read a few sentences which are mere fragments of the entire argument.

"History proves indisputably that a superior and an inferior race cannot live together practically on any other terms than that of master and slave, and that the inferior race, like the Indians, must be expelled or exterminated."

"I was born among the Negroes of the South, have spent many years in the study of their natural and civil history, and feel confident in the prediction that they are doomed to extermination which is being cruelly hastened by the unwise action of a party that will not study and comprehend the subject it is dealing with. The Negro has an instinctive and unconquerable antipathy to steady agricultural labor, and must therefore be gradually supplanted by the whites, whose energy, industry and intelligence will rule in this and all other important pursuits."

"The blacks, like the American Indians, Tartars, and other nomadic races, are instinctively opposed to agricultural labor, and no necessity can drive them to it. Slavery is the normal condition of the Negro, the most advantageous to him, and the most ruinous, in the end, to a white nation.

"After removing your Bureau and the troops, I see but one duty remaining for you to perform, and that is, to assist us in feeding and clothing colored paupers. The old, the infirm, the women and children, the worthless vagrants, will form a burden that we are unable to carry. As long as women and children were property, and the unproductive child was one day to be a profitable producer, the owners could afford to feed women and children that constitute one-half this population. All this is now changed, and the capital of the South is no longer adequate to provide for such enormous charity.

"I say, then, that you have brought this state of things upon the South, in spite of remonstrances, and you must 'pay out' or see the victims of your policy starve."

Such was the prophecy of the leading ethnologist whose science taught and still teaches a large section of our people. He declared that the Negro could never be fit to live on equal terms with the white, to be anything more than a slave, because nature had given him nine less cubic inches of brain than she had given us of the Germanic stock. Now consider how this gloomy prophecy with all its science has been exploded. The Negro freedman has proven that he is willing to work, and that he is capable of thrift. He has supported himself and his dependent children and invalids. He has been the chief agricultural producer in the southern states, and in twenty years had doubled the cotton crops, and nearly quadrupled other farm products. By the last census 34% of the white people of Massachusetts owned their homes, but 37% of the Negroes of Virginia owned theirs.

Negroes own more than 177,000 farms in the country,

and operate 581,000 more, a total of 38,250,000 acres. In Mississippi and Louisiana there are more Negro farm owners than white. Thus a large part of the agricultural South is coming into the possession of Negroes. As to pauperism there are over a third more white paupers per thousand than Negro. And meanwhile the less than four million Negroes when Dr. Nott was writing have increased to about ten million. That does not look like extermination.

RACE DIFFERENTIATION—RACE CHARACTERISTICS

Livingston Farrand, M. D.

Professor of Anthropology
Columbia University

I have been asked to say a word here this morning on the general problem of race differentiation and race characteristics from the anthropological standpoint; and I am afraid I must indulge in what I wish particularly to warn against, and that is, generalities, because of the short time at my disposal.

If there is one subject in the discussion of which caution is to be observed it is this very theme which we are here to consider. There is no field of investigation in which generalization is more frequent or in which it is more often unjustifiable. At the same time during recent years when the problem has been actively investigated it would seem that certain trends of authoritative opinion have appeared, some of which it may be worth mentioning.

Let me add another word of explanation, and that is with regard to the term "race." I believe that word to be at the present time in hopeless disrepute. We do not know what it means and are unable to agree upon an arbitrary definition of it. While I shall use the word I wish it distinctly understood that I use it in a general and popular sense.

When we are speaking of race differentiations we are not necessarily dealing with permanent or invariable differences, but are simply using a convenient term and vehicle of discussion. Any classification of so-called "races" becomes a pure matter of description, and, from the point of view of accuracy, physical characteristics afford perhaps the most defensible basis for such classification. At the same time, no matter what physical factor may be taken as a criterion, we find that the variations within the groups so defined are so wide as to cause overlapping in every direction and make definite conclusions difficult, or even impossible. This difficulty is illustrated as well by the criterion of skin color as any other, and yet it is probably the most commonly used and certainly the most convenient of any of the physical factors suggested as a basis.

It has been hoped that the accurate measurements of the skull would afford material of a character so definite that a safe foundation might be afforded, and yet in recent years it has become evident that even so relatively stable a character as the shape of the head exhibits variability of the most pronounced type. It has recently been shown that among the Jews, distributed as they are throughout the civilized world among different racial groups of all kinds and yet retaining to a marked degree an *apparent* purity of stock or race, the head form varies according to the environment, that is, it tends to approach the head form of the group among which the given Jews in question may reside.

All this by way of caution as to the difficulty in reaching a classification acceptable to even a small number of anthropologists or others competent to form an opinion.

The problem which more immediately concerns a conference such as this is the question whether it is possible from an anthropological standpoint to classify groups of men upon a psychological basis. In other words, are there permanent mental or psychological differences which will permit definite group differentiations?

In attacking this problem we are forced to deal with the mental expressions and mental reactions of men in groups which naturally exhibit themselves as customs. That there are differences in such mental expressions no one can deny. The Australian savage differs from the German and the Negro differs from the Chinaman, the problem being to determine upon what these differences of mental expression ultimately rest.

It is commonly held that two possible lines of explanation are open. These psychological differences may represent actual differences in mental organization, which in turn represent different degrees of mental evolution, or, they may be the results simply of the mental experiences of the individuals which constitute the groups in question. In other words, there may be differences of mental capacity representing the grades of development, or they may be the result of differences of environment and training which modify the mental contents of the individuals of the groups, but which do not necessarily represent any appreciable difference in mental organization or development.

The question as it is ordinarily put resolves itself into this: Does civilized man represent a higher stage of mental evolution than the savage?

In considering the problem we must remember that we are apt to form our judgments very largely upon differences of culture, and in so doing we are apt to confuse a perfectly obvious *cultural* evolution with a perfectly problematical *mental* evolution. The two terms are by no means synonymous. It seems clear that one may accumulate the products of men's minds and hand over the material so assembled to the child, which process carried on throughout a given group will necessarily produce a higher stage of culture without making necessarily one iota of difference in the initial mental capacity of the individuals so treated.

There is another point which perhaps ought to be considered as preliminary, and that is the light which anatomical considerations might throw upon the question. I am very glad to see that this aspect of the subject is to be discussed by one far more qualified than I—Professor Wilder—who is to follow me this morning. But for fear Dr. Wilder will not say just what I would like him to say let me speak for a moment of my own point of view.

If we consider the brain, which it is agreed is the anatomical factor most closely concerned with the question, from the point of view of size, weight, and complexity, we shall find undoubtedly certain differences existing between the brains of one racial group and those of another racial group. It is true that a large series of brains from Central African Negroes compared with an equal number taken at random from Central Europe would show a slightly less degree of size and weight in the African brains as compared with the European. On the other hand this would simply mean that the great mass of the two series so compared would coincide and it would only be in the extreme members of the two groups that any recognizable differences would appear. Stated in another way it appears that the variation within each group is so wide that for nearly every African brain there would be a corresponding European brain so far as size and weight are concerned. This being the case it seems obvious to any candid mind that inferences with regard to the development of groups so treated are extremely dangerous and that inferences with regard to the mental development of the groups so considered are entirely unjustifiable. This is naturally still more true from the fact that we are quite unable to state the correlation which may exist between mental capacity and brain development.

Let us not, however, fall into the similar error on the other side and deny with equally indefensible dogmatism that such differences as do exist have no significance and can be left entirely out of account. The only statement which it seems to me will bear the scrutiny of candid science is that thus far the investigations of this point are negative.

Returning again to the question of psychology it is obvious that there are differences of mental expression in different groups of men. On the other hand if we inspect these groups broadly we find it equally obvious that the general mental processes are similar or identical. If we attempt to decide whether the mental capacity, so-called, of one group of men is greater or less than that of another group of men we are met at once by the difficulty of determining a criterion by which we may judge such differences. I have never yet been able to find psychologists who could lay down exact standards applicable to field observation which could be used in solving this particular problem.

If we inspect the more obvious conscious processes such as sense perception there is certainly no difference to be described. The acuteness of vision of the Englishman and the American Indian are perfectly comparable. The Indian or Australian may exhibit marvellous powers in following trails or in tracking game, but it has been shown that this skill is based not upon increased visual acuteness but upon training in perception of certain stimuli through a life of necessity. The same principle holds true of differences which present themselves in the other senses.

If we consider certain of the more complex mental processes in which it might be thought that differences in kind might exist it seems to me that the results of analysis are similar to those obtained in an inspection of the simpler processes.

18

It has often been held that the ability to inhibit impulses is a mark of high mental development, whether individual or racial. Inhibition expresses itself ordinarily in the individual as self-control, the ability to check impulse to action of one sort or another, and it has been assumed that the savage or more primitive individual is characterized by a lack of self-control; that is that he tends to yield to the impulse of the moment whatever it may be. It would seem that an inspection of the evidence would not bear out this contention. It is clear that the self-control exerted by the individual in any group is to a large extent a conventional one. He is taught to inhibit along certain lines in certain groups, and what is conventional or good form for the individual in one group is not necessarily so in another. You and I are taught from childhood to inhibit certain reactions and expressions and as we grow older such repression becomes habitual with us. The same is true of the savage.

It was impressed upon the American Indian from his earliest days that if he were put to torture by his enemies he was not to give way to any expression of pain, but to endure the utmost agony without a moan. Should the crucial test arrive he seldom failed to meet the demand, but that same Indian in the bosom of his family would exhibit behavior of the most childish character over an injury of the slightest kind. Where there is no necessity or conventional call for inhibition he does not exhibit it.

Further, the savage often exhibits self-control under conditions where you and I would be incapable of it. The Eskimo may be in a state of semi-starvation with seals lying all around him on the ice, yet if for religious reasons a taboo has been placed upon these seals the Eskimo will starve to death before he will kill and eat one. You and I would not do that. Your religious prejudice and mine would disappear in the face of hunger and the innate nutritive impulse. What is true of the Indian or the Eskimo is true of the Negro, Australian, and every other primitive group. The direction which the inhibition of impulse or self-control shall take is dependent largely upon training and convention, and so far as we can see does not exhibit particular differences of degree or strength.

Probably equal attention has been given to the question of the evolution of ethics. It seems clear that there are two problems involved in this discussion, one the evolution of ethical standards as such, and the other the degree of conformity to these standards, whatever they may be, as exhibited by different racial groups. We find, of course, that different standards exist in different groups and that what is right in one group may not be right in another, or what is right at one time may not be right at another, but the point which concerns us, it seems to me, is chiefly the degree of conformity to the standards recognized by particular groups rather than the standards themselves. Viewed in this way the strictness of conformity to ethical standards among savages is quite comparable to that which exists among civilized man.

Time does not permit discussion of this point in detail, but ethnology is full of evidence to that end.

If I may be permitted to sum up these discursive remarks I have been making and to express what I believe is the point of view of an increasing school of anthropologists, it is that the *apparent* differences of mental capacity in different groups of men are probably to be assigned much more to the contents of the minds of the individuals of these groups than to any inherent differences of mental capacity which would indicate a recognizable difference of mental evolution.

I don't believe it is possible, I don't believe it is right to say that there are no differences of degree of evolution between different groups. Such a thing, of course, is possible theoretically and I believe it is to a certain extent actually. It is reasonable to suppose that a certain selection has operated which would have produced possible differences of mental organization, but let us not forget that the time during which such special selection can have operated is extremely short and that further it is equally possible that a similar selection may have been going on in savage groups where conditions have not been favorable for the development of a culture to the point which we call civilization.

Now I will inhibit. In conclusion I wish to bring out this one point—that it is absolutely unjustifiable to assert that there is trustworthy evidence for the view that marked differences of mental capacity between the different races exist; that if they exist they are certainly of a much slighter extent than would appear from hasty observation. On the other hand it is equally unjustifiable to assert that no differences exist.

A very wise remark was made a few years ago by an American sociologist when he said: "It may be true that blood will tell, but we must not be too hasty in saying just what it is that the blood tells, or which particular blood it is that speaks."

THE BRAIN OF THE AMERICAN NEGRO

Burt G. Wilder

Professor of Neurology and Vertebrate Zoology in Cornell University

[The address on this subject, as delivered extemporaneously at the Negro Conference, was prepared within a necessarily limited time. For present publication it has been recast and much new material has been added, mainly in the form of Notes, Tables, Illustrations, and a List of Publications referred to.]

Do any physical characteristics of the brain of the American Negro warrant discrimination against him, as such?

The American Negro is on trial, not for his life but for the recognition of his status, his rights and his opportunities. At this, as at most other trials, experts disagree. Fortunately, against none of them can be laid the charge of being influenced by the hope of "power or pelf." But prepossessions may result from circumstances, and even in science the "personal equation" must be reckoned with. Approximate impartiality is claimed by me because, on the one hand, as a believer in the derivation of the human body from some anthropoid stock, I incline to minimize the differences between man and the higher apes; and because, on the other, during both my army and university experiences, there have been occasions when I was tempted to exclaim, "Yes, a white man is as worthy as a colored man—provided he behaves himself as well."

To the initial question my reply is, in brief: Respecting the brains of American Negroes there are known to me no facts, deductions, or arguments that, in my opinion, justify withholding from men of African descent, as such, any civil or political rights or any educational or industrial opportunities[1] that are enjoyed by whites[2] of equal character, intelligence, and property.

To the above negative testimony I add the affirmation, based upon personal observation, that the title to such rights and opportunities was earned during the Civil War by the general conduct of soldiers of African descent, by their valor, by their initiative under trying conditions, and by their deliberate self-sacrifice for the sake of a principle.

The consideration of special aspects of the subject may well be prefaced by two general declarations respecting the African race by the late Professor Huxley;

---

1. Among the matters here named should not be interjected questions of social or marital relations; they are no more germane than religious affiliations. The case has been well stated by President Kilgo (*South Atlantic Quarterly,* vol 2, p. 383): "Social equality is everywhere a matter of individual choice. Each man chooses his companions and on the grounds of personal congeniality. The Negroes are not socially equal among themselves, neither are the white people, and the wild cry that the time will come when one man will be forced to associate with another contrary to his wishes is a nightmare and a political hocus-pocus." Let me say here that among the cleanest—physically and morally—men that I have known have been some of African descent. As to the interdiction of legal intermarriage, but for the tragic aspect of the whole subject there would be something ludicrously inconsistent in the horror at the mere entrance of an African male into a southern mansion (otherwise than in a menial capacity) when far closer relations of occupants of those mansions with African females are attested by the numerous mulattoes, some of them rightly bearing "first family" names.

2. To avoid complications all the statements in this address refer to males only. Unless otherwise stated, by *whites* are meant male Caucasians of the United States or Canada; by *Negroes,* Afro-Americans, men of African descent in the same countries.

they exemplify the clearness, consistency, conciseness, and correctness that characterize his writings; if they lack completeness (the last of the "five C's" that I have for many years commended to my pupils) it is because nearly half a century has elapsed since they were penned, and because he had had no opportunity of observing the modern American Negro and his treatment by certain individuals and communities:

"Middle Africa exhibits a new type of humanity in the Negro, with his dark skin, woolly hair, projecting jaws, and thick lips. As a rule, the skull of the Negro is remarkably long; it rarely approaches the broad type, and never exhibits the roundness of the Mongolian. A cultivator of the ground and dwelling in villages; a maker of pottery, and a worker in the useful as well as ornamental metals; employing the bow and arrow as well as the spear, the typical Negro stands high in point of civilization above the Australian."—Essays, vol. 7, p. 233.

"It may be quite true that some Negroes are better than some[3] white men; but no rational man, cognisant of the facts, believes that the average Negro is the equal, still less the superior, of the average white man. And, if this be true, when all his disabilities are removed, and our prognathous relative has a fair field and no favour, as well as no oppressor,[4] it is simply incredible that he will be able to compete successfully with his bigger-brained and smaller-jawed rival, in a contest which is to be carried on by thoughts and not by bites."—Essays, vol. 3, p. 67.

---

3. Were this valiant champion of justice alive to-day and familiar with the character and achievements of leading Afro-Americans he might change "some" in the first line to *many,* or even echo the opinion of the former editor of the *South Atlantic Quarterly,* vol. 2, p. 299.

4. Not to adduce more savage methods, is *op*pression—or merely *re*pression—the appropriate term for the exclusion of a University professor of African descent from a public library for which he and his fellows are taxed?

In the foregoing paragraph Huxley meant, of course, that prognathism is more common among Africans than Caucasians; but every observer knows that it is by no means either constant with the former or absent with the latter. In fact, by far the most prognathous human being that I ever saw was a trained violinist from the interior of Europe. In the museum of Cornell University the following incident was witnessed by me: Among a party of visiting youths were a "low-down" Negro and a rough Irishman. From opposite directions they chanced to approach a stuffed chimpanzee. As each caught sight of it he raised his finger and pointed, with a grin, at the other fellow. The resemblance was not a matter of race, but, as Prof. Farrand has remarked, of individual culture.

It will be noted that, like all other scientists known to me, Huxley recognizes the African as one of the human races. The contrary view is doubtless entertained by some, but as yet, so far as I am aware, it has been publicly formulated only by a clergyman of the Lutheran denomination, Rev. G. C. H. Hasskarl. In the subtitle of his little book, "The Missing Link" (1898), is the query, "Has the Negro a Soul?" His own reply seems to be contained in the following passages:

"The Negro is a separate and distinct species of the *genus homo* from Adam and Eve"; p. 29. "The Negro is not a human being"; p. 28. "He is inevitably a beast and as a beast entered the ark"; p. 29. "The difference between the white man immortal and the Negro soulless"; p. 33.[5]

"The Missing Link" is evidently based upon narrow and prejudiced interpretations of the literal sense of certain passages of Scripture, and the arguments would

---

5. A letter from Mr. Hasskarl, dated Williamsport, Pa., Dec. 24, 1909, says: "For want of time I am unable at present to enter into a discussion of your soul-problem concerning the

probably appeal only to persons of comparatively limited knowledge and influence. But no such mitigating circumstances apply in the case of a liberally educated writer who had every opportunity for ascertaining the facts and whose statements would undoubtedly and materially affect the numerous readers — intelligent but uninformed—of a popular periodical.

In order to avert further misapprehension—of which there has been too much already—this matter shall be told, so far as practicable, in selections from a correspondence between Mr. Owen Wister[6] and myself. Interpolations are in brackets.

My second letter to Mr. Wister was dated Dec. 29, 1905, and ran as follows:

"I beg to acknowledge the receipt, yesterday, of the reply to my queries of the 20th. Pardon my persistence, but there is more to be said. In your [very interesting] story, "Lady Baltimore," in the *Saturday Evening Post* of Dec. 9th, the relator, evidently a man of at least average intelligence and discrimination, when shown three skulls, viz., of an Aryan (ordinary white), of a gorilla, and of a South Carolina 'nigger' (to quote a word that I would not otherwise employ), recognizes

---

Negro. In about two months there will be out a publication of mine on Christian Pedagogy. In it I am treating of the souls of both man and beast, and when you have examined the same you will understand what I mean by the adjective 'soulless' when speaking of the Negro in contrast to the white man."

"The Missing Link" was discussed by several colored clergymen in the *New York Tribune* for May 28 and 29, 1899.

As reported in the *Tribune* for February 4, 1910, the Rev. E. H. Richards, for thirty years a missionary in Uganda, Africa, believes that the Negro is descended from "one of several brothers of Adam."

6. Strictly speaking the correspondence was with the private secretary of Mr. Wister. That the latter evidently did not know me from Adam—or Ham—was, of course, a blow to my self-esteem; it may also be interpreted as signifying that, while the scientist must have romance, the novelist may—or sometimes thinks he may—dispense with science.

a 'gap' between the first and the other two, but between those two a 'brotherhood, a kinship which stares you in the face'; he avows that 'the difference in their names was the only difference he saw between them,' *e.g.*, between the skulls of a gorilla and of a South Carolina Negro.

"To my inquiry as to whether this comparison was intended to indicate merely your own impression or was based upon some anthropologic authority, you reply that 'it incorporates no special knowledge, but only information of the ordinary kind which is to be found in any museum of anatomy or academy of natural sciences.'

"Before expressing my own opinion permit me to call your attention to the following paragraph from the first scientific account of the gorilla in the *Boston Journal of Natural History,* vol. 5, Aug. 18, 1847. Its author, Professor Jeffries Wyman of Harvard University, was noted for his freedom from prejudice, for his accuracy of observation, and for his clearness of expression. He says (using *orang* as a general name for the tailless or anthropoid apes, and thus as embracing not only the true orang but the chimpanzee and the gorilla) : 'Any anatomist who will take the trouble to compare the skeletons of the Negro and the orang cannot fail to be struck at sight with the wide gap which separates them. The differences between the cranium, etc., in the Negro and the Caucasian [here used, like your Aryan, as a term for the white race] sinks into comparative insignificance when compared with the vast difference which exists between the conformation of the same parts in the Negro and the orang.'

"Under Jeffries Wyman I began to compare the skulls of men and apes in the fall of 1859, nor has my interest in them ceased merely because it is now surpassed by my interest in their brains. Not to risk the 'mixing up of things,' which Mrs. Carlyle so aptly denounced as 'the great bad,' let us agree that (1) There are racial differences; and (2) When all things are considered, the whites have advanced further than the blacks from our [presumed] ape-like ancestors.[7]

"But I believe the present state of our knowledge warrants the following propositions: First, in an assemblage of adult male skulls of the apes and the various human races a child would unhesitatingly separate the men from the apes, and might go further and set apart the gorilla by reason of the prominent bony crests. Secondly, among three skulls such as are indicated in your story the expert anatomist might recognize one as presenting certain features that are more often found in Africans; but even to him, and, *a fortiori,* to the layman, these peculiarities, as compared (to use Wyman's phrase) with the 'vast difference between the Negro and the gorilla, would sink into comparative insignificance.'

"The validity of these propositions may be ascertained from any comparative anatomist or from the collections in your city, and I venture to express the hope and belief that you will feel called upon to make immediate retraction of the contrary statements in your story.

"At best, however, a month would have elapsed since the original publication. Hence, failing to receive within a reasonable time assurance of your intention to take such action, unwelcome as the task would be, I could not evade what seems to me the obligation to try

7. This is also warranted by the following passage from the same paper of Wyman: "It cannot be denied that the Negro and the orang [meaning the tailless apes, as above] do afford the points where man and the brute, when the totality of their organization is considered, most nearly approach each other"; 1847, p. 441. In this connection, however, it should be added that, in respect to the location of the *foramen magnum,* the hole in the base of the skull where the brain is continuous with the spinal cord, Wyman found the North American Indian to rank lower than the Negro; 1868, p. 447. Likewise should not be overlooked the fact that the hair of apes and monkeys is straight and thus resembles that of the Negro less than it does the curly locks of many Caucasians.

to arrest the further diffusion of the scientific error and the political venom that characterize the passages in question." At a meeting of the American Anthropological Society, Dec. 28, 1905, I laid the matter before that Society in a paper.

Under date of Jan. 3, 1906, was given this assurance: "Mr. Wister will investigate the matter at the earliest opportunity, and if he find that what he said is not justified by sufficient scientific authority he will take every step in his power to set the matter right."

In the February number of *Alexander's Magazine,* as part of an Appendix to the Garrison Centenary address as printed in the preceding number, and under the caption, "A Novelist's Needless Error," I said: "Even if the misstatement is qualified or retracted in the book-form of "Lady Baltimore," the atonement will be far from adequate. I print this note (and trust it may be reprinted) as an authoritative correction of an injurious scientific error."

Under date of Feb. 24th, in the acknowledgment of the receipt of a reprint of the Address and Appendix above mentioned, it is stated: "Mr. Wister is very glad you have taken the step of personally correcting his overstatement. It seemed to him that the personal and public retraction which you demanded was out of proportion with the error. The passage stands corrected after having been submitted to Mr. Arthur Erwin Brown. It is a middle course between the extreme one originally taken in Mr. Wister's sentences, and the other extreme one taken in your own."

The passage in question, on p. 171 of "Lady Baltimore," is now as follows:

"There was a similarity of shape, a kinship there between the three, which stared you in the face; but in the contours of the vaulted skull, the projecting jaws, and the great molar teeth—what was to be seen? Why, in every respect that the African departed from the Caucasian, he departed in the direction of the ape."

Neither the emendation, nor the disclaimer in the preface of a "feeling against the colored race," seem to me to constitute reparation for the original wrong. For one cultivated and discriminating reader of the volume there are probably ten who have been directly or indirectly misled by the statement in the periodical. In my judgment, especially in view of the declaration quoted above from the letter of Jan. 3rd, "he will take every step in his power to set the matter right," the author was and still is bound to publish an explicit retraction in the same periodical. A nearly equal responsibility rests upon the conductors of the periodical.

The episode narrated above has an indirect as well as direct significance. So far as known to me no other person protested against the original allegation. This might be taken to signify merely indifference. But it may also be interpreted as indicating a general lack of accurate knowledge respecting the skulls of apes and of races of men. Since such specimens are readily obtained and easily prepared, and since they are exhibited in all large museums and represented in comprehensive works, there may fairly be assumed an even greater and more widely spread ignorance concerning the contents of these bony cases. Such brains are far less easily obtained and preserved; in museums they are less common and less accessible; they are very complex (the human brain presents at least five hundred features, parts, and combinations of parts visible to the naked eye and provided with one or more names); and fewer anatomists devote themselves to their study and comparison.[8] Hence it may not be out of place to offer a few elementary statements, general and particular.

8. It is encouraging to note that the reorganized Wistar Institute of Anatomy in Philadelphia has made early and special

1. Among the brains of vertebrates, from the lamprey up to man, under multifarious differences of detail, there is recognizable such unity of type as to furnish one of the strongest arguments for the belief that the higher or more specialized forms have been evolved from lower or more generalized.

2. The animals most nearly resembling man in structure are the three true apes, orang, chimpanzee, and gorilla. Among the points in common are the total absence of a tail and the presence of the cecal appendix.[9]

3. When human and ape brains are compared, whether from the several external surfaces (Figs. 5, 6, 7) or after division into right and left halves as shown in charts not reproduced here[10] the resemblances are so numerous and impressive that anyone who accepts the general doctrine of evolution can hardly resist the conclusion that men and apes have been derived from some common stock.

4. Nevertheless, and irrespective of absolute size (the smallest human brain [680 grams or 24 ounces] outweighs the largest ape brain [500 grams or 17 ounces], see Tables I and III), between the brains of all animals, including the apes, and those of all human races, so far as examined, the differences are several,

provision for neurologic research by experts. Even more imperative, in my judgment, is the acquirement by all persons of a certain amount of personal familiarity with brains representing the principal vertebrate groups. Upon several occasions I have urged that this practical work begin in the primary school, and during the last five years I have specified, as most favorable for beginners, the brain of the Acanth shark (*Squalus acanthias*) commonly known as the "spiny or horned dog-fish"; see the paper, 1907, and the references in it.

9. In these respects and some others man is also approached by the gibbons, but in other respects these are evidently less removed from the tailed monkeys than are the other apes.

10. Some of these charts included the entire brain; but the figures here given represent only the cerebral hemispheres, the parts related most directly to consciousness, volition, and intellectuality.

considerable, and practically constant. So far as I know there has never been examined a brain respecting which there could be a doubt as to its human or ape nature.[11]

5. At various times and by various writers certain differences have been alleged to exist between African and Caucasian brains, *viz.,* color, the presence of the "ape-fissure" (named "pomatic" by me in 1889, and "lunatus" by G. Elliott Smith later), the greater frequency and distinctness of the postrhinal fissure (to the presence and morphologic significance of which I called attention at the American Neurological Association in 1885), the absence of the "sulcus frontalis mesialis," the brevity of the Sylvian fissure, the lateral extension of the occip ital fissure, the general simplicity of fissuration, less development of the frontal portion of the callosum (the great band of fibers connecting the two cerebral hemispheres, Fig. 13), ventral concavity or lateral flattening, or both, of the prefrontal lobe, less relative size of the entire frontal lobe, and less weight of the entire brain.

6. So far as I have been able to ascertain from the writings of others and from my own observations, none of the features above enumerated is comparable in extent and significance with the differences between all human and all ape brains; none is constantly present in the African, and each occurs sometimes in the Caucasian.

Before considering some of these alleged differences more in detail I state my conviction that, even were they more numerous, more considerable, and more constant, they should not invalidate conclusions legitimately derived from conduct indicative of lofty ideals and of the ability and disposition to act in accordance with them.

---

11. This remark applies, of course, only to forms now living. Speculation as to the conditions in *Pithecanthropus erectus,* the fossil primate of Java, would be out of place here.

Color.—Since the brain, like the rest of the central nervous system, is primarily derived from the same embryonic layer as the skin, and since part of the membrane covering the sheep's brain is black, and with the "spoon-bill sturgeon" (Polyodon) the fatty connective tissue surrounding the brain is richly pigmented, one might not unnaturally expect to find the African brain of a darker hue. Such was claimed to be the case in a mulatto by Laboulbène in 1849, but it was probably an individual peculiarity. Museum specimens present many shades of color due to the nature of the preservatives employed. For example, in the Cornell University collection the darkest brain (3531) was from a physician and poet, while that of a Negro (3808) is one of the lightest.

Most of the other alleged characteristics of the African brain[12] could not be discussed without technicalities out of place on this occasion.

Fissural or gyral simplicity.—The surface of the cerebrum is smooth in early stages of development and remains approximately so with the lower monkeys; with the higher monkeys and with the apes the arrangement is simpler than in man. Hence, upon the supposition that the African race, as a whole, has made less progress than the Caucasian from ancestral and infantile conditions, the cerebral fissures of Negroes might be expected to present a less degree of complexity and a more obvious symmetry between the right and left sides.

The literature of this subject has been reviewed by

12. It will be interesting to ascertain from the careful examination of many well prepared African brains whether there is any resemblance to the lower mammals, including the apes, in a greater absolute or relative size of the olfactory bulb, or of the part variously called thalamic fusion, middle commissure, and massa intermedia; my own observations do not look that way, but they are too few for generalization.

Mall who has also compared many brains of the two races; he makes the two following statements: "Brains rich in gyri and sulci (fissures) of the Gauss type,[13] are by no means rare in the American Negro"; p. 24. "With the present crude methods the statement that the Negro brain approaches the fetal or simian [ape] type more than does the white is entirely unwarranted"; p. 20.

In this connection my own experience, while not perhaps unique, may be related as exemplifying the undesir- ability of drawing conclusions from a small number of cases. One of the first brains obtained entire for Cornell University was that of an unknown and presumably obscure mulatto of medium color. It was hardened within the skull so that the contours, both general and special, were perfectly preserved. Although the fissures were peculiar in some respects they and the intervening gyres were far simpler than any known to me and were employed as the basis of diagrams that have served my pupils and those of others in the elucidation of the more complex usual conditions.

Later acquisitions showed how unwise it would have been to regard this mulatto brain (Fig. 3) as a type of the mixed black and white, or to assume that all Caucasian brains are more complex, and that still greater simplicity prevails with the full blacks. The next three African brains obtained by us (3118, 3808, and 2912) presented various degrees of the usual fissural complexity, and the last of these, from an illiterate janitor, apparently full black, is comparable with that of a mathematician and philosopher (3334, Fig. 8).[14]

---

13. Gauss was a German mathematician and his cerebral fissures were unusually complex.

14. So altruistic was this man, and so keen his sense of justice, that he would surely rejoice to know that his brain had contributed in any way to the increase of knowledge and the righting of wrong.

On the other hand, the cerebrum of Chauncey **Wright,** another philosopher and mathematician (Fig. 4), distinctly recalls that of the mulatto in what may be termed its "Egyptian" style of architecture as contrasted with the more common "Corinthian" style. Finally, and to complete this series of warning paradoxes, in the Cornell collection the nearest approach to the Wright-mulatto type is made by the brain of Ruloff (965) who, although a murderer, was fairly educated and interested in linguistic problems; his skull is the thickest that I ever saw, while the thinnest is that of the mulatto; Figs. 1 and 2.

Alleged prefrontal deficiency in the Negro brain.— The anterior portion of the cerebrum, sometimes distinguished as the prefrontal lobe, includes a part, at least of the "anterior association areas" which are supposed to subserve the higher psychic faculties, especially reason, judgment, and self-control or voluntary inhibition. In apes and monkeys this region is both absolutely and relatively smaller than in man (Fig. 10, orang and baboon), and although the other contours are more or less rounded there is a distinct ventral concavity. Upon information of Hrdlicka and at the suggestion of Mall, Bean undertook to determine whether the brains of American Negroes are deficient in this important region, and examined many specimens to that end. His observations and conclusions were published in the same year, 1906, in the *American Journal of Anatomy* and in the *Century Magazine* for September; these periodicals will be distinguished as *A. J. A.* and *Century;* the article in former is fuller but that in the latter is less technical and more likely to be accessible to the laity.

On p. 412 of the *A. J. A.,* Bean claims, mainly if not wholly from the form and size of the frontal lobe, that "the Negro brain can be distinguished from the Cau casian with a varying degree of accuracy according to the mixture of white blood."

In a later number of the same journal Mall reviews (1909) the several statements of Bean in the light of an extensive series of his own observations. He says (p. 18) that the flattening over the anterior association area may be seen in most full-blood Negroes, certainly in more than one-half. A mixed lot of sixty Negro brains and thirty white were assorted correctly in seventy-five per cent. of the cases. A more satisfactory test would be the assortment of larger and equal numbers of the two races. No one would be justified in the inference that the determination could be made with any such certainty as that between the brains of all apes and those of all human races.

In the *Century* article, however, p. 782, Bean makes this sweeping declaration:

"The size and shape of the front end of the brain is different in the two races, being smaller and more angular in the Negro, while it is larger and more rounded in the Caucasian. Fig. 1 shows vertical sections taken through the frontal lobes between 1.5 and 2 centimeters from the front end of the brain of a Negro, and between 2 and 2.5 centimeters from the front end of the brain of a Caucasian.[15] The section of the Caucasian brain is larger and more circular than that of the Negro, not exhibiting

_____

15. Since the frontal lobe commonly tapers forward a section nearer the front end will usually be smaller than one further back; hence it was only just in Bean to state (as in the above extract) that the Negro brain was cut nearer the front end. Unfortunately, however, this qualification is not repeated in connection with the figure itself, which is on the following page. Now figures are so much more impressive than descriptions that probably most readers would infer that the two sections were made at the same level and would interpret the difference in size to the disadvantage of the Negro. This unwarranted interpretation seems to have been made in an editorial in *American Medicine* (April, 1907. p. 197) which stigmatizes the enfranchised Negroes as "an electorate without brains."

36

the narrow projecting sides and pointed tips above and below."

From the foregoing and from the accompanying figures it might naturally be inferred that the two forms of the prefrontal lobe are constant and characteristic of the two races. That this is not the case may be seen from my Figs. 10 and 11. These are photographic reproductions of transections of eight primate[16] cerebral hemispheres in the prefrontal region. In order that the sections might be at the same structural level in all, there was adopted the "base-line" employed by Bean (*A. J. A.*, p. 404, said by him, p. 354, to have been suggested by Mall), passing just below the hinder end of the callosum and just above the precommissure ("anterior commissure") and usually coinciding nearly with the greatest length of the hemisphere. By means of a frame the several sections were made at right angles with this line at a level half-way between the end of the hemisphere and the precommissure.

The sections of the orang and the baboon (both unusually intelligent individuals) display decided inferiority as to both form and extent. Between the two jurists there is little difference, but what there is seems to favor him of the higher character and greater self-control (2870). With the white philosopher (3334) and the illiterate black janitor (2912) the ventral excavation is nearly equal, but the latter presents a dorso-lateral flattening that is wholly absent from the former.

The white murderer (3335) equals the other three whites in form and surpasses them in area. There is a slight ventral concavity which does not appear at all in the mulatto thief (3118); in the latter, moreover, the slight dorsal concavity is deceptive, and due to the break-

---

16. This word relates to any member of the order Primates, including man, apes, monkeys, baboons, marmosets, and lemurs.

ing off of a slightly attached piece; the natural outline at that point is rounded.

Surely no detailed arguments are required to expose the fallacies lurking in any comparisons of small numbers of specimens. Bean's collocation of the transections of the prefrontal lobes of *a* Negro and *a* Caucasian (even if made at the same level) as if they represented a constant racial difference, is no more conclusive as to the two races than would be my collocation of the white, 3652, with the Negro, 3118, as proving the cerebral superiority of the African race, or the collocation of the righteous judge (2870) with the executed murderer (3335) as a guide to our relative esteem for the criminal classes and those who pass upon their misdeeds.

Alleged less size of the entire frontal lobe in the Negro.—According to Bean (*A. J. A.,* p. 377) the whole region in front of the central fissure ("fissure of Rolando") is smaller in the Negro than in the white. Mall reviews the evidence and concludes (p. 13) that "it is incorrect to say that the frontal lobe of the Negro is lighter than that of the white."

In the concluding paragraph of his article Mall emphasizes the need of more material and better methods as follows:

"In this study of several anatomical characters, said to vary according to race and sex and intellectuality,[17] the evidence advanced has been tested and found wanting. It is found, however, that portions of the brain vary greatly in different brains and that a very large number of records must be obtained before the norm will be found. For the present the crudeness of our methods will not permit us to determine anatomical characters due to race, sex, or genius, which if they exist are completely masked by the large number of

17. In a private letter Dr. Mall authorizes me to interpolate this word, not included in the original.

marked individual variations. The study has been still further complicated by the personal equation of the investigator. Arguments for difference due to race, sex, or genius will henceforward need to be based upon new data, really scientifically treated, and not on the older statements."

Brain-weight.—Just how much significance should be ascribed to the weight of the brain is by no means certain; it is, however, a subject of natural and general interest upon which statements are not always correct and interpretations not always sound. The following nine tables have been compiled from the latest reliable sources accessible to me. An effort has been made to construct them so as to tell their own story. The notes and comments are numbered to correspond with the lines in each Table, whether or not the lines are numbered.[18]

Upon the present occasion it has been found impracticable to take into account several very important qualifying factors, viz., the absolute and relative size of the cerebrum alone, the thickness and histologic structure of the cortex, and the correlations with stature, body-weight, age, and disease; these last four topics have been ably discussed by Donaldson, 1895, 1908, and 1909.

General conclusion.—So far as I can determine from the publications of others and from my own observations, the utmost that can be said at present is:—(1) The average brain-weight of obscure American Negroes is a little (about 2 ounces, or 50-60 grams) less than that of obscure American whites, and (2) With Negroes more frequently than with whites does there occur prefrontal deficiency. But (1) Many Negro brains weigh more than the white average, and many white brains weigh

---

18. The ounce is the avoirdupois, sixteen to the pound, equivalent to 28.349 grams; in reducing from one system to the other the ounce is reckoned as 28.35 grams. Conversely, 100 grams equals 3.52 ounces, roughly three and one-half.

less than the Negro average; (2) Some white brains present lateral or ventral depression of the prefrontal lobe, and some Negro brains do not. As yet there has been found no constant feature by which the Negro brain may be certainly distinguished from that of a Caucasian; whereas either of them is at once distinguishable from the brain of an ape, and would be by a dozen or more points of structure, even if they were of the same size.

For the determination of possible racial peculiarities larger numbers of brains of both races should be examined with impartiality and by more exact methods. Particularly useful would be the brains of persons of African descent who have achieved eminence in any respect.[19] Yet, even if it should appear that certain features or conditions occur more frequently in the Negro, so long as these conditions are not constant in the Negro and so long as they sometimes occur with whites, and even with those who are morally and intellectually superior, the greater average frequency in the Negro should not be interpreted to the disadvantage of worthy individuals of that race.

TABLE I.—APPROXIMATE BRAIN-WEIGHTS OF SOME ANIMALS LARGER THAN MAN

	Pounds	Ounces	Grams
Gorilla, the largest ape	..	17	500
Bison, four years old	..	18	529
Some whales	5	80	2265
Rhytina, extinct "sea-cow"	5	79	2242
Elephants	10	160	4500

1. Of five adult male gorillas Turner found (1897, p. 451) the largest to have a cranial capacity of 590 cubic centimeters. Employing as the coefficient .87 (stated by Spitzka [1907, p. 218] to

19. Should the Afro-American leaders of to-day bequeath their brains to some institution that would preserve them properly and study them fairly and thoroughly the next generation might find the statistics of brain-weight telling a very different story Copies of a "Form of Bequest of Brain" may be obtained from the writer.

be that of Manouvrier), gives as the weight of its brain 513 grams; but as the average cranial capacity of the five was 494 c.c., the round number, 500, is here provisionally adopted. The adult male gorilla is estimated by Owen (1868, p. 144) to weigh nearly 200 pounds, considerably more than the average man.

2. The bison, although young, had probably gained the full size of both body and brain; the latter is said by Hrdlicka (1905, p. 98) to have weighed 529 grams, something more than a pound.

3. From the nature of the case the brains of large cetaceans have seldom been weighed fresh. According to Bischoff (1880, p. 23), that of an individual 75 feet long weighed 1942 grams after hardening in alcohol, and he estimates the fresh weight as 2816; even if this be excessive the general weight assigned in our Table is certainly moderate.

4. The Rhytina inhabited the shores of Bering's Strait; it resembled the manatee, or "sea-cow," but was much larger; no brain was actually weighed, but Bischoff states (p. 24) that from a cast of the cranial cavity the weight was estimated by Brandt at 2242 grams; see also Smith, p. 347.

5. Like the manatee's, the brain of the rhytina was probably simple, with large ventricles. But the elephant's brain is very substantial and richly convoluted. The average weight of five brains enumerated by Bischoff (p. 23) is 4485 grams, in round numbers 4500, or nearly ten pounds.

Although three of the above-named animals surpass man in the absolute weight of the brain, their bodies are so gigantic that the relative weight falls far below the human, about one to forty-five; in this respect, also, man surpasses the bison, the gorilla, and indeed most animals larger than a cat. But, as may be seen from the Table in Hrdlicka's paper (1905) the brain is relatively larger than in man with some small monkeys (marmosets), with some birds, with several rodents, and with a shrew-mole. In all these, however, the cerebrum is nearly or quite devoid of convolutions.

It appears from the above statistics that any statement as to the comparative brain-weight of animals and man must be accompanied by several qualifications.

Number	Race	Country	Status	Ounces		Grams
1	27	Cauc.	U. S. & Can.	Notable	53	53.25	1510
2	14	"	Gt. Britain	"	52	52.24	1481
3	24	"	U. S.	Soldiers	52	52.06	1475
4	108	"	Various	Notable	52	51.95	1473
5	70	"	"	"	52	51.92	1472
6	3	Eskimo	N. A.	Various	51	51.39	1457
7	20	Cauc.	France	Notable	51	51.35	1457
8	38	"	Ger. & Aus.	"	51	50.75	1439
9	2,000	"	Europe	Various	49	49.38	1400
10	51	"	U. S.	Obscure	47	47.26	1341
11	381	African	"	Soldiers	47	46.73	1325
12	51	"	"	Obscure	46	45.57	1292
13	70	"	"	"	45	45.39	1287
14	10	"	Africa	"	43	42.64	1209

1, 2, 4, 5, 7, and 8 are derived from the "List of the brain-
weights of 108 notable men" constituting Table I of the paper
(1907) by E. A. Spitzka.[29] In that Table the individuals are
named in the order of their brain-weight, beginning with the
highest. In using it I have found it convenient to number the
individuals, serially, 1-108; then, in a separate column, to pre-
fix the numbers under which the cases are discussed at greater
or less length upon pages 107-209. From these fuller accounts,
and with the coöperation of the author were corrected the following errors: the brain-weight of E. C. Seguin (40) should
be 1502, not 1505; that of Oliver (65), 1416, not 1418; that of
Agassiz (43), 1514, not 1495, and that of Zeyer (95), 1310, not
1320. It was not noticed at first that No. 31 is Taguchi, a
Japanese anatomist; his brain, however, weighed 1520 grams,
coming thus within the middle fifty of the series and not affecting materially the average or the comparison with other
series.

I. These include twenty-five residents of the United States
and two Canadians; from the standpoint of climatic environment there seems to be no reason for separating them. The
superior brain-weight, as compared with the fourteen
British notables, may have accompanied greater stature
and body-weight, as remarked by Hunt (1869, p. 53), in the
case of soldiers of this country and of Europe; but such data

20. The worthy son of an eminent father, E. C. Spitzka; were
the latter not fully occupied in other directions his knowledge
and his nature (as exemplified in his almost single-handed defiance of the *vox turbae* respecting the mental status of the
assassin, Guiteau) would naturally enlist him in behalf of the
still oppressed Afro-American.

are not available with these notables. The average brain-weight of these twenty-seven American notables is nearly identical with that (1513) of the nine eminent Caucasians in Spitzka's Table A, p. 304.

3. This item is from Hunt. The superior brain-weight may be compared with that of the obscure whites in line 10.

5. These seventy were chosen by lot for comparison with an equal number of obscure Negroes in line 13 (from Table VI.). The 108 serial numbers were written upon small cards together with the corresponding brain-weights. The cards were shaken thoroughly in a box. The drawer, blindfolded, drew out seventy, and their average weight was ascertained; the cards were shaken a second time and the drawing repeated. The first average was 1481, the second, 1462. The average of the two is 1471.5, tabulated as 1472, or 51.9 ounces, nearly identical with that of the entire 108.

6. These three Eskimo weights, as found, respectively, by Chudzinski, Hrdlicka, and Spitzka, to be 1398, 1503, and 1470, are recorded by the last named (1902, p. 31). The average is interestingly high, and may be correlated with the necessity for strenuous effort for self-preservation in high latitudes, but the number is too small for generalization.

9. According to Bean (*Century,* p. 782, the averages for males and females were obtained from several sources respecting 4000 European Caucasians; I have assumed that the sexes were equally represented.

10 and 12. These items are from Bean's *Century* article, p. 782, and are presumably based upon his Table I in the *A. J. A.* So far as I can judge, in most cases the brains were not weighed until after they had been subjected to a preservative, either before or after removal; see under Table V. Without attempting to account for the sudden drop from the European average (excepting upon the supposition that the latter included eminent as well as obscure individuals), Bean's average for the obscure Africans coincides nearly with that derived from the seventy in the next line, and as an average may be accepted even if doubt exists respecting individuals.

11. These 381 Afro-American soldiers are from Hunt, 1869, p. 51; see Table VII. The higher average, as compared with the obscure negroes, recalls that of the white soldiers in line 3. As indicating the selection of individuals more or less superior as to mental and physical endowment it illustrates the force of an argument in favor of peace, *viz.,* the undesirability of exposing such potentially efficient citizens to wounds and death.

13. These are from Lamb, as stated under Table V.

14. From Waldeyer, 1894, p. 1220; see Table 4. The contrast between the two averages recalls the possibility of climatic influence as with the 27 North American notables; it is regarded by Waldeyer (1894, p. 1221) as indicating an interesting and difficult problem probably involving several factors; he speci-

fies only one, *viz.,* the mixture of white blood; but from the right column of Table 5 it will be seen that the average brain-weight of the 29 full-blacks is 1283 grams, 74 above that of the native Africans and only 4 below that of the 70 of all grades.

TABLE III.—BRAIN-WEIGHTS OF SELECTED INDIVIDUALS OF VARIOUS RACES, COUNTRIES, AND STATUS

	Name; race; country; status	Ounces		Grams
1	Turgenev; Russian writer; eminent......	71	70.90	2012
2	Negro; nearly white; U. S.; obscure....	56	55.97	1587
3	Negro, black; U. S.; obscure	55	55.02	1560
4	Kishu; Eskimo; chief of tribe	53	53.01	1503
5	Native East African	51	51.14	1450
6	Hottentot; unusually tall	50	50.00	1417
7	J. E. O.; mathematic teacher; philosopher	50	49.94	1416
8	G. F.; black janitor; illiterate	44	44.09	1250
9	Gall; German phrenologist	42	42.25	1198
10	X. Y. Z.; jurist, politician; drunkard ...	39	38.90	1103
11	Native East African	36	36.40	1030
12	D. L.; white watchman	24	24.00	680
13	F. W. B.; congenital idiot	13	12.52	355

1. From Spitzka, head of his Table I.

2. and 3. From Lamb; see Table V.

4. From Hrdlicka and Spitzka; see Table II, 6.

5. From Waldeyer; see Table IV, first entry.

6. From Wyman (1862); the man was 5 ft. 5½ in. high, unusual for that race; I saw him alive and took part in the dissection.

7. Prof. James Edward Oliver of Cornell University, a profound thinker, an enthusiastic teacher, and of the loftiest character. His brain was represented and described by me in 1889 and 1900.

8. George Field; apparently full black; illiterate; janitor of the Zeta Psi Chapter House at Cornell University; said to have been faithful and worthy.

9. From Spitzka's Table I, near foot of list.

10. X. Y. Z., said to have been an able lawyer and successful politician in a large city; see p. 57 and fig. 5.

11. See last item of Table IV.

12. So far as known to me this is the smallest brain of a rational man; it has been kindly loaned to me by Prof. J. H. Larkin of Columbia University, and will be described at the coming General Meeting of the American Philosophical Society. Compare the exceptionally small native African brain mentioned in the note under Table IV.

13. From Macnamara and Burne, 1903. The brain is said to have presented ape-like features, but it was unmistakably human. See also Smith, p. 463.

TABLE IV.—BRAIN-WEIGHTS OF TEN NEGROES FROM GERMAN
EAST AFRICA (WALDEYER)

Original Number	Ounces	Grams	Original Number	Ounces	Grams
12	50.15	1450	6	43.20	1225
10	45.30	1285	8	40.50	1150
4	45.00	1275	3	39.70	1125
2	44.10	1250	1	37.10	1050
11	44.10	1250	7	36.40	1030

Average of the ten, 42.64 oz., equals 1209 grams.

These cases are from Waldeyer, 1894. In the original there are twelve brains. The weighing was done in Africa by Dr. Steudel and recorded in grams, here reduced to ounces. Neither Waldeyer, in publishing the weights, nor Duckworth in quoting the average (1904, p. 436), seems to have been impressed with the preponderance of round numbers. Accepting them as given they have been reduced to ounces, and ten have been rearranged so as to bring the higher weights above, but retaining the numbers of the original list. Two have been omitted. No. 5 was not weighed till after hardening; the fresh weight was then computed at 907, markedly below the fresh weights known for the ten here included. No. 9 was from a youth of 18, dying of sepsis and greatly emaciated; the fresh weight is given as 780 grams, reduced to 630 by hardening. The fresh weight is so low as to suggest subnormal intelligence, perhaps imbecility, that invalidates comparison with what seem to be representative individuals; were these more numerous its inclusion with them might be warranted, as would be the inclusion of the exceptionally small brain of "D. L." (Table III, item 12) among hundreds or thousands of whites. The omission of the two doubtful cases above mentioned raises the average weight of these ten native Africans from 1148 to 1209, sixty-one grams or a little more than two ounces; but this still leaves considerable and probably significant margins between it and 1287 for the obscure Afro-Americans, and 1325 for the United States soldiers of African descent; the inclusion of the two doubtful cases would increase the size of the margins.

45

Various Shades		Dark Mulatto		Black	
Serial No.	Grams	Serial No.	Grams	Serial No.	Grams
50	1446	81	1417	1660	1560
62	1432	52	1417	89	1530
33	1261	88	1375	58	1502
Av. of 3 1380		82	1375	37	1502
Mulatto		69	1361	55	1417
83	1446	73	1361	2521	1395
68	1403	27	1318	56	1375
59	1403	22	1304	91	1361
42	1361	87	1304	30	1361
44	1318	45	1304	2522	1350
41	1304	57	1290	43	1332
98	1304	23	1290	63	1332
32	1261	79	1276	28	1304
71	1247	85	1247	66	1276
24	1247	49	1247	61	1276
18	1148	64	1219	40	1261
94	1120	77	1205	15	1261
Av. of 12 1297		47	1191	2912	1250
Light Mulatto		70	1162	84	1219
96	1247	51	1162	75	1219
36	1191	14	1134	92	1191
7	1105	20	1120	93	1191
Av. of 3 1181		Av. of 22 1276		35	1191
Nearly White				80	1162
21	1587			29	1148
				67	1077
				95	1063
				17	1063
				1661	1040
				Av. of 29	1283

In view of the rarity of available records of the brain-weights of individual American Negroes I have added to the 65 males in Lamb's series the only other five known to me, *viz.*, 2912, the illiterate black janitor mentioned under Table III, and numbers 1660, 1661, 2521, and 2522 of Bean's series; as I understand his Table I and the statements on pp. 358-9, these four are the only ones that were weighed fresh and before the injection of a preservative that might affect the weight.

46

	Num- ber	Racial Admixture	Averages		Totals
			Ounces	Grams	
1	1	Nearly white	56.00	1587	1587
2	3	Light mulatto	41.65	1181	3543
3	12	Mulatto	45.75	1297	15562
4	3	Various shades	48.68	1380	4139
5	22	Dark mulatto	45.00	1276	28079
6	29	Black	45.25	1283	37209
	70	Totals	45.39	1287	90119

4. The few individuals included under this vague title have
been given an intermediate place.

6. The greater brain-weight of the full-blacks than of those
with slight admixture of white blood is interesting and has been
commented upon by others; see Table VII; its cause and significance are yet to be determined.

Number	Racial Admixture	Ounces	Grams	Totals
25	¾ White [quadroon]	49.05	1390	34750
47	½ " [mulatto]	47.07	1334	62698
51	¼ " [sambo]	46.54	1319	67269
95	⅛ "	46.16	1308	124260
22	1-16 "	45.18	1280	28160
141	Black	46.96	1331	187671
		46.73	1325	504808

This is based upon the "Ethnographical Table" of Hunt, 1869,
pp. 40-54. The records were made under the direction of Sur-
geon Ira Russell, 11th Massachusetts Volunteers, during the
Civil War. The original weights are given in ounces; the reductions to grams here offered coincide with those of Work
(1906), p. 27, note). In the *Century* (1906, p. 782) Bean under-
takes to reproduce Hunt's Table, but the average weights are
stated in grams only; for the three-fourths white his number,
1390, is the same as ours; for the whites (see Table X) his
number is three grams higher, while for all the other grades of
the colored the numbers are three, four or five lower; probably the reductions were made in haste and not verified. The
Century article of Bean (1906) contains (p. 782) an independent
column of weights for several grades of color to which he
refers in the *A. J. A.,* p. 410, as warranting practically the same
conclusions as those of Hunt. See, however, under Tables II
and V.

As to the degrees of racial admixture, in the absence of
statement to the contrary it is assumed that the fractions in
the second column represent declarations as to parentage made

by the soldiers and recorded at or subsequent to enlistment. In estimating the extent of admixture from the degree of coloration two observers are apt to differ.

TABLE VIII.—COMPARISON OF BRAIN-WEIGHTS OF OBSCURE AFRO-AMERICANS WITH THOSE OF OBSCURE EUROPEANS

	Cau-casians	Afri-cans
Total number	559	70
Below the lowest Caucasian, 1018.............		00
Above the highest African, nearly white, 1587..	24	
Above the highest black, 1560..................	29	
Approximately equal, within 5 grams...........	55	55
Unrepresented within 5 grams: 1261 (3); 1250 (1); 1247 (4); 1191 (4); 1148 (2); 1105 (1)		15

The Africans are the same seventy as in Tables V and VI. The Europeans are from the first part of Table I of Bischoff's series (1880) following p. 171. For fifty-five of the seventy African weights were found in the European series counterparts, either exact or differing not more than five grams. Of the fifteen for which no such approximate counterparts occur in the European series there are three of 1261 grams; one of 1250; four of 1247; four of 1191; two of 1148, and one of 1105.

This and the following table substantiate the eminently clear statement of the case by Prof. Farrand, p. 17.

TABLE IX.—NEARLY IDENTICAL BRAIN-WEIGHTS OF 27 NOTABLE WHITES AND 27 OBSCURE NEGROES SELECTED FROM 108 OF THE FORMER AND 70 OF THE LATTER; THE HEAVY-FACED NUMBERS ARE FROM FULL-BLACKS.

Serial Number [19 higher]	Notable Whites	Obscure Negroes	Serial Number	Notable Whites	Obscure Negroes
20	1590	1587	84	1373	1375
23	1560	**1560**	85	1370	1375
29	1530	**1530**	86	1365	**1361**
38	1503	**1502**	87	1361	**1361**
40	1502	**1502**	88	1358	1361
60	1445	1446	91	1349	**1350**
62	1437	1432	92	1332	**1332**
64	1418	**1417**	96	1300	**1304**
65	1416	1417	97	1290	1290
67	1415	1417	99	1276	**1276**
72	1403	1403	100	1272	**1276**
73	1403	1403	101	1257	**1261**
76	1395	**1395**	103	1250	**1250**
83	1374	**1375**		[24 lower]	
			Averages	1390.52	1391.04

48

This is based upon Spitzka's Table I, "List of brain-weights of 108 notable Caucasians of various nations," and Bond and Lamb's list of brain-weights of 65 obscure Afro-Americans plus the 5 mentioned in connection with Table V. The serial numbers of the notables are given at the left of each column. At the head of the first column "19 higher," in brackets, indicates that so many notable weights were greater than any of the obscure; at the foot of the second column "24 lower" indicates that so many obscure weights were less than the lowest notable. The gaps in the serial numbers indicate notables for which there were no approximate counterparts among the obscure.

Of course a natural and fairer comparison would have been between equal numbers of the same general status; but there is available to me no such series of obscure white Americans. It is not surprising to find that 24 of the obscure Negro brains are lighter than the lightest of the notables; that 19 of the latter are heavier than the heaviest of the former; or that, among the higher weights, are omitted more than fifty serial numbers because there were no approximate counterparts among the Negroes. But surely it is worthy of note that in 11 cases there should be absolute equality; that in the remaining 16 the difference should not exceed 5 grams (one-sixth of an ounce); that the excess should be so evenly distributed that the averages are practically identical; and that of these 27 obscure men of African descent whose brains approximately equalled in weight those of 27 notable whites, 16, more than half, were full-blacks.

TABLE X.—SOME STATISTICS OF THE FIFTY-FIFTH REGIMENT OF MASSACHUSETTS VOLUNTEER INFANTRY, COLORED; THE COMMISSIONED OFFICERS WERE WHITE; ONE, GEORGE T. GARRISON, WAS A SON OF HIM WHOM GOLDWIN SMITH (1892) CALLED A "MORAL CRUSADER"

980	Total number of enlisted men
430	Mixed blood
550	Apparently pure black
247	Had been slaves
319	Could read and write
477	Could read only
184	Could neither read nor write
52	Were church-members
219	Were married
112	Died from disease
54	Killed in action or died from wounds

Table XI.—Abridged Record of the Enlisted Men of the Fifty-fifth Massachusetts Volunteer Infantry, Colored.

1863 Jan. 26. Authority of Secretary of War for enlistment on same terms as white soldiers, $13.00 per month, plus $3.00 allowance for clothing
" May 12, Enrolment began
" July 25, Service in South began
" Nov. 28, Refused $10.00 per month, pay of laborers, less $3.00 for clothing
" December, Refused balance, $6.00, from Massachusetts
1864 Persistent refusal of lower pay
" June 18, One shot for resisting officer
" July 2, "Rivers Causeway," took initiative in action; out of about 350, 7 killed and 19 wounded
" Oct. 7, First payment, after more than 14 months
" October, Celebration decorous; all loans repaid; by Adams Express alone, over $60,000.00 to families
" Nov. 30, "Honey Hill"; out of about 360 engaged, 32 killed and 88 wounded
1865, Sept. 23, Mustered out

American Negroes in the Civil War

I was asked to speak of the brain, and was also told that I might emphasize my opinion of the African race by a few words upon a different subject. It was my good fortune to enter the medical service of the army in July, 1862, and to be commissioned in the spring of 1863 as one of the medical staff of the Fifty-fifth Massachusetts Infantry (colored); see Tables X and XI.

I think the youths of to-day, white or black, do not realize under what circumstances those two regiments, the Fifty-fifth and the Fifty-fourth, went into the field. They went not only against the prejudice of the community and the indifference of the government, but in the face of Confederate declarations to the effect that if captured they should be treated as runaway slaves.[21] The situation is outlined in the following extract from Col. Henry Lee's "Shaw Monument Address," 1897, pp. 58-59.

"No one can appreciate the heroism of the officers and soldiers [of the colored Massachusetts regiments] without adding to the savage threats of the enemy the disapprobation of friends, the antipathy of the army, the sneers of the multitude here; without reckoning the fire in the rear as well as the fire in front. One must have the highest form of courage not to shrink from such dismaying solitude."

The composition and record of the Fifty-fifth are indicated in Tables X and IX, below.

After our regiment had been arduously engaged in the siege of Charleston, S. C., in the summer of '63, for some months, the paymaster appeared with orders to pay the enlisted men ten dollars a month, the wage of laborers, less three dollars a month for clothing![22]

The Fifty-fourth and the Fifty-fifth had been enlisted in Massachusetts under orders of the Secretary of War, which are on record, and under authority from Governor Andrew, and with the full understanding upon the part of everyone concerned in Massachusetts, and with the understanding of the men themselves, that they were to be treated in every respect like white troops, the pay of which was thirteen dollars besides the regular uniform. The men consulted and decided that they would not accept ten dollars a month. That was on the 28th of November.

---

21. The actual treatment of colored prisoners is described by Emilio, "Appendix." For various official Confederate utterances see "War Records," vol. 22, p. 965; Serial No. 117, p. 946, and Serial No. 118, p. 940; the last is a joint resolution of the Confederate Congress, May 1, 1863, to the effect that the white officers of colored troops should be put to death; this threat was never carried out. See also extracts in *The Nation*, September 28, 1899, p. 241.

22. For various accounts of the matter of the pay of these and other colored troops see Fox (1868), Emilio (1894), Hallowell (1897), Lee and Kennard (1897), Pearson (1904, vol. 2, pp. 94-120), and my Garrison address (1905). So moderate a man as Jeffries Wyman—whose most violent expletive, "By George," was heard by me only once— wrote me as follows under date of May 26, 1864: "All you say about the pay of the soldiers puts the Government in a very shabby light; its members are disgracing themselves in the eyes of the world."

In December, knowing the circumstances, knowing that a good many of them were without other means, that some were married, and that others had mothers or fathers or friends that they wished to help — the Legislature of Massachusetts passed a law to the effect that provisionally the state should make up the difference between what was offered by the United States and what the men felt they had a right to receive.

The State Commissioners and the officers of the regiment urged the men to accept this as a compromise for the sake of their families. Again they met and consulted and decided, almost unanimously, that they would not take the money. They said, "We have not enlisted in this war for pay; we are here to fight for our country and for the honor of our race, and we will take nothing until the United States government pays what is our due, and what we were promised when we enlisted."

Months passed. The men continued to work, to watch to fight—and to wait for justice.

In the meantime a few of them had lost control of themselves—some of us whites lose control of ourselves—and one resisted an officer. For his offense I saw that man shot. The government that could not find law to pay him otherwise than as a laborer could nevertheless find law to shoot him as a soldier.

During this payless period both regiments had fought bravely. The attack of the Fifty-fourth upon Fort Wagner (see Emilio, Hallowell, Lee and Kennard) could not be surpassed for heroism. Col. Shaw and the other officers gallantly led and were as gallantly supported by the enlisted men.

If it be said, Negro soldiers merely follow their officers and do what they are told, I reply that on one occasion[23] when our officers supposed the order was to

23. At Rivers Causeway, James Island, near Charleston, S. C., (July 2, 1864,), as described by Fox (1868, pp. 29-32) and myself

retire, the enlisted men rushed forward, captured two field-pieces, and fired them upon the retreating foe. If, again, it be said, it is natural for the male animal to fight, and physical courage is shared with the brutes; then I reply that these men displayed moral courage and self-restraint under the very trying conditions described above in respect to their pay. Nor was this all. When at last the United States government came to its senses; when at last it decided to do justice, fourteen months after their service began,[24] then these men received their money, and they had a celebration not nearly as boisterous as that in a college town after the victory of an athletic team.

To refute the declaration that the Negro, when he gets his money, squanders it, I add that out of that first payment to the Fifty-fifth Massachusetts there was sent home to the wives and families and friends in Massachusetts by the Adams Express Company alone—not counting other express companies, and other means of conveyance—there was sent home by these soldiers, many of whom had been slaves, $60,000![25]

Nor is this all. Some months earlier, at the urgent request of the soldiers, the officers had received their pay. Then we had loaned various sums to them, and out of what had been loaned during that year and a quarter by the officers, in sums ranging anywhere from fifty dollars down to twenty-five cents, there is not on record or in recollection a single instance in which payment was not made and made promptly. I will not say what white soldiers would have done under similar circumstances. But could they have behaved any better?

(1906, p. 24). A comparable action of white enlisted men is said to have occurred at Missionary Ridge.

24. With the Fifty-fourth the service in the field began two months earlier.

25. See Fox (1868, p. 37); my letter of Oct. 16, 1864, says $65,-000.00, but Fox is probably correct.

Being myself merely a student of natural history, I have appealed to several professors of *un*natural history, and have failed as yet to learn that, taking into account all the circumstances of the payment of the two colored Massachusetts regiments, there has ever been a finer example of self-renunciation and sacrifice for the sake of what was regarded as a principle.[26]

Shall we now deny civil and political rights, and educational and industrial opportunities, to men merely because they are black, because the average weight of their brains is a little less, and because a certain region of the brain may be more frequently less developed, when two thousand of their fellows, nearly half a century ago, could manifest not merely the highest kind of physical courage, but as high a kind of moral courage, as has been chronicled in the history of the world?

---

26. Should the writer be spared until other conditions permit he will regard it as a sacred duty to put in a form accessible to others his observations and impressions of the military and personal conduct of the members of the Fifty-fifth Massachusetts as recorded in daily letters, all of which have been preserved.

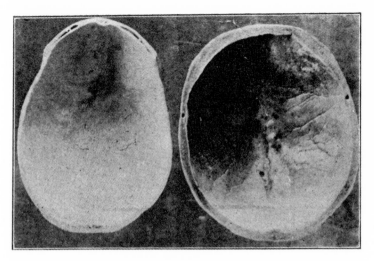

I   2

Fig. 1, No. 322, Obscure Mulatto.

Fig. 2, No. 965, White Murderer, Ruloff.

The specimens represented above were photographed together and reduced to a little less than one-third natural size. They are the "skull-caps" (calvas or calvaria), as sawn off the top of the skull for the removal of the brain. That of the mulatto was cut at a lower level than the other; had the latter been sawn at the same level some portions of the cut edges might not have been quite so wide, but the rest of the skull was not preserved and the question cannot be settled; even allowing for this the white skull is much thicker than the mulatto; both are exceptional; see p. 34.

As remarked by Huxley in the passage quoted on p. 23, the African skull is usually narrow, and the one figured above may be fairly representative; the Caucasian skull seems to me unusually short and rounded. In the latter the small hole at either side is artificial. In Fig. 1, at the upper end. corresponding with the forehead, are seen the slight frontal sinuses between the inner and outer tables of the skull; they do not appear in the other skull, but may have existed at a lower level.

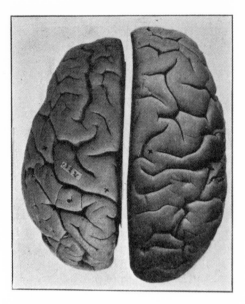

3   4

Fig. 3, No. 322, Obscure Mulatto.

Fig. 4, White Philosopher and Mathematician, Chauncey Wright.

Dorsal (upper) aspects of two cerebral hemispheres, photographed together so as to be a little less than one-half natural size. With both there is an unusual simplicity of the fissures and the intervening gyres (convolutions), as mentioned on p. 34. The more common conditions appear in Fig. 5.

The mulatto brain was hardened in the skull and hence retains its original form. That of Wright evidently underwent some distortion after removal, but—as appears when viewed at a different angle—the front (upper, in cut) end was unusually square. The mulatto brain was not weighed fresh; Wright's weighed 1516 grams, 53.50 ounces.

Both brains present fissural peculiarities which are discussed in my "Handbook" article, Figs. 762 et seq., and Fig. 770. In Fig. 4 the Central fissure is interrupted by an isthmus marked by a black x; in Fig. 3 the continuous fissure passes behind the two similar marks and the paper strip bearing the number.

56

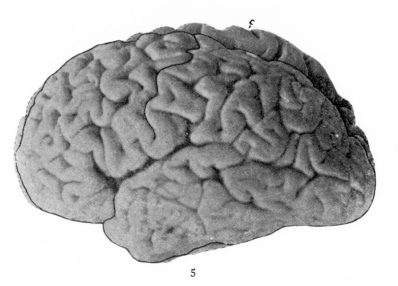

5

Fig. 5. The continuous black line is the outline of the left cerebral hemisphere of No. 3652; the interrupted line is the outline of the right hemisphere of No. 2912. They were photographed together so as to be about one-third natural size. On 2912 the Central fissure is marked C; on 3652 its course is shown by the undulating black line; the shorter line at the lower margin represents part of the Sylvian fissure.

These are the opposite halves of the cerebrums of two very unlike persons. The right half is from G. F., an illiterate black janitor. The left from a white jurist and politician. As an ally of Tammany Hall he probably condoned, if he did not encourage, the race riots in this city in the spring of 1863 when the first northern colored troops enlisted in spite of Democratic opposition. If so, we may charitably ascribe his conduct to sharing the general belief that every Negro's brain is so small as to unfit him for citizenship or even for military service. Yet the brain of the black janitor weighed 5 ounces more than that of the white jurist (Table 3), and now, when the left half of the latter is held against the right half of the former so that the lower margins coincide, at nearly all other points the black's outline may be seen beyond the white's. Let us hope that X. Y. Z. now rejoices that at least one of the blunders of his life has been rectified after his death.

57

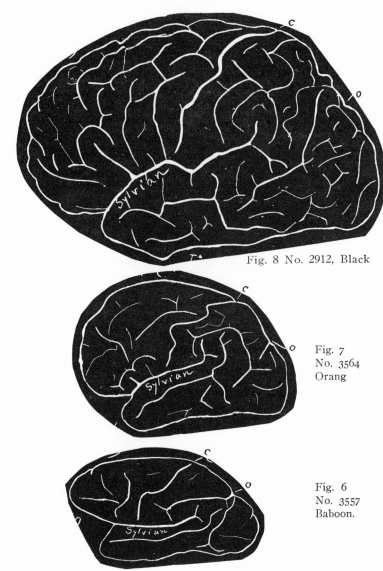

Fig. 8 No. 2912, Black

Fig. 7
No. 3564
Orang

Fig. 6
No. 3557
Baboon.

All about two-thirds natural size.

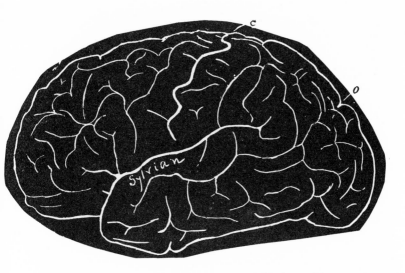

Fig. 9, No. 3334, White Philosopher and Mathematician.

This and the figures on the opposite page are from photographs of blackboard diagrams (themselves based on photographs) of the left cerebral hemispheres, reduced to about two-thirds natural size. The Sylvian fissure is named on all; the upper end of the Central is indicated by C; the O indicates the location of the Occipital fissure, most of which is on the mesal (median or inner) aspect. There is an obvious community of general pattern of fissuration, by which any of them would be recognized as a primate rather than a dog, sheep, or other mammal. The orang was unusually intelligent, and the baboon was highly trained in a show. The black was the illiterate janitor, G. F., mentioned on p. 34; he and the white philosopher are included in Table III. The two present individual differences of fissuration, such as might occur between two whites or two blacks, but no racial differences recognized by me. Transactions of the frontal lobes are represented in Figs. 10 and 11.

Jurists

Upright   Unscrupulous

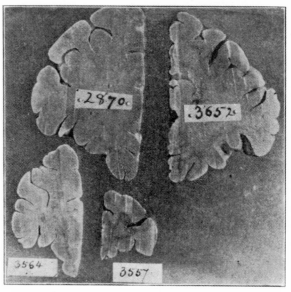

Orang   Baboon

Fig. 10. Transections of the frontal lobes of a baboon, No. 3557, an orang, No. 3564, an "upright judge," No. 2870, and an unscrupulous, intemperate jurist-politician, No. 3652. These specimens and the four represented on the opposite page were prepared in the same manner as described on p. 36 and photographed all together so as to be reduced in the same degree to about five-sevenths of the natural size.

The sections of the orang and the baboon (both unusually intelligent individuals) display decided inferiority as to both form and extent. Between the two jurists there is little difference, but what there is seems to favor him of the higher character and greater self-control (2870).

Mulatto thief   White murderer

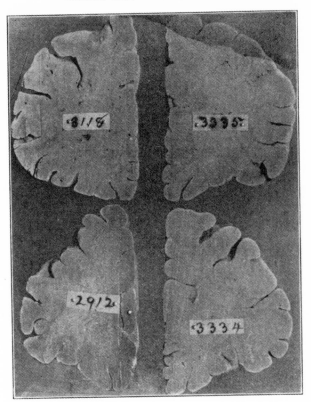

Black janitor   White philosopher

Fig. 11. With the white philosopher (3334) and the illiterate black janitor (2912) the ventral excavation is nearly equal, but the latter presents a dorso-lateral flattening that is wholly absent from the former.

The white murderer (3335) equals the other three whites in form and surpasses them in area. There is a slight ventral concavity which does not appear at all in the mulatto thief (3118); in the latter, moreover, the slight dorsal concavity is deceptive, and due to the breaking off of a slightly attached piece; the natural outline at that point is rounded.

For general commentary see p. 37.

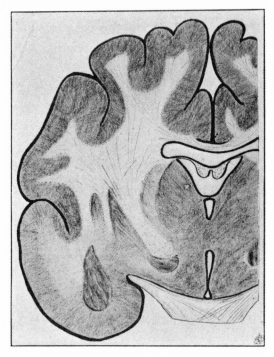

Fig. 12. Transection of Cat's Brain, enlarged. This and
Fig. 13 on the opposite page are to be considered together. Both
are from drawings kindly loaned by Spitzka; similar reproductions form part of Plate XVI of his paper, 1907. They are semi-
diagrammatic representations of the main features of the two
cerebrums when cut across at nearly the same level. The meson
(middle plane) corresponds with the cleft nearer the right of
each figure, most of that half being omitted to save space. The
two are represented as of the same size. The darker marginal
zone represents the cortex; this and the other dark areas are
cinerea or gray matter, composed in part of nerve-cells; the
light areas represent alba, composed of nerve-fibers. The black
lines in the alba indicate the general direction of the fibers. The
callosum (indicated by C on Fig. 12) is a thick sheet of fibers
connecting the two cerebral hemispheres at the bottom of the
mesal cleft.

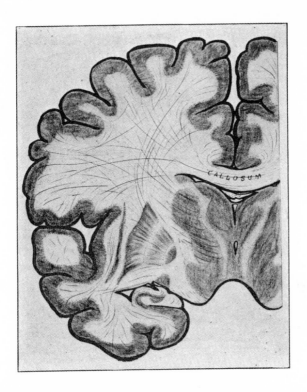

Fig. 13. Transection of Human Brain, reduced. For the general features see the description of Fig. 12.

Contrary to the general impression the human brain has a relatively larger amount of the alba (white matter) composed of fibers connecting (a) the cerebral cortex with the lower parts of the brain and so, indirectly, with the body; (b) the right and left hemispheres, the callosum; (c) the several portions of the same hemisphere, the association fibers; p. 34. Man's superiority is supposed to be correlated with the development of these association fibers and of the cortical areas with which they are connected. Spitzka found the callosum unusually large in an eminent naturalist, Joseph Leidy, and thinks there is evidence of correlation in this respect as between individuals and perhaps races.

List of Publications Referred to

Bean, R. B., 1906.—The Negro brain. The *Century*, September, 1906, pp. 778-784, with map, figures and tables. (Unless otherwise indicated by *A. J. A.* this article will be understood as referred to since it is the more likely to be accessible to readers of the present publication.)

——1906.—Some racial peculiarities of the Negro brain. *American Journal of Anatomy,* vol. 5, No. 4, September, 1906. Pp. 353-432, with many tables, charts, and figures.

Bischoff, T. L. W. v., 1880.—Das Hirngewicht des Menschen. *O.*, pp. 171, with about as many pages of Tables.

Boas, F., 1906.—Commencement Address at Atlanta University, May 31, 1906. *Atlanta University Leaflet, No.* 19.

Carnegie, Andrew, 1908.—Scotch and Negro Progress Weighed. Remarks, as reported in the *New York Tribune,* December 20, 1908.

Donaldson, H. H., 1895.—The growth of the brain. Contemporary Science Series, *O.*, pp. 374. London.

——1908.—The weight of the brain as modified by nutrition and disease. Read before the American Neurological Association. May, 1908. (Manuscript copy.)

——1909.—Some conditions modifying the interpretation of human brain-weight records. Read at the General Meeting of the American Philosophical Society, April 23, 1909. (Manuscript copy.)

Emilio, L. F., 1894.—A Brave Black Regiment. History of the Fifty-fourth Massachusetts Volunteer Infantry, 1863-1865. Second ed., *O.*, pp. 452, portraits and maps. Boston.

Fox, C. B., 1868.—Record of the service of the Fifty-fifth Massachusetts Volunteer Infantry. Privately printed by the Regimental Association, Cambridge. *O.*, pp. 194, 1868.

Hallowell, N. P., 1897.—The Negro as a Soldier in the War of the Rebellion. Read before the Military Historical Society of Massachusetts, Jan. 5, 1892. *O.*, pp. 29, Boston, 1897.

Hasskarl, G. C. H., 1898.—The Missing Link, or the Negro's Ethnological Status. *D.*, pp. 176. Reprinted from the *Eastern Lutheran.* Published by the author, Philadelphia.

Hrdlicka, Ales, 1905.—Brain-weight in vertebrates. *O.*, pp. 89-112. Reprinted from *Smithsonian Miscellaneous Collections,* Quarterly Issue, vol. 48.

Hunt, Sanford B., 1867, 1869.—The Negro as a soldier. *Journal of Psychological Medicine and Jurisprudence,* October, 1867, p. 182. Also in the *Anthropological Review,* vol. 7, pp. 40-54, January, 1867. [From the footnote to p. 40 it may be inferred that this paper was printed originally as a report to the U. S.

Sanitary Commission, but I have been unable to locate it among its publications.]

Huxley, T. H., 1865.—Emancipation, black and white. Collected Essays, vol. 3, Science and Education, 1894, pp. 66-75.

——On the African Negro. Methods and Results of Ethnology, Essays, vol. VII, 233.

Laboulbène, 1849.—*Comptes Rendus des Séances et Mémoires de la Société de Biologie de Paris*, p. 6.

Lamb, D. S., 1894.—Some brain-weights in the Negro race. *American Anthropologist*, N. S., vol. 6, pp. 364-366. For original records of 1865-6, see under Table V, *supra*.

Lee, H., and Kennard, M. P., Committee, 1897.—The Monument to Robert Gould Shaw. *Q.*, pp. 98, Boston.

Macnamara, N. C., and Burne, R. H., 1903.—The Cerebrum of a Microcephalic Idiot. *Journal of Anatomy and Physiology*, N. S., vol. 17, pp. 258-265, 6 figures.

Macnamara, N. C., 1908.—Human speech. *The International Scientific Series*, vol. XCV. *O.*, pp. 284. London.

Mall, F. P., 1909.—On Several Anatomical Characters of the Human Brain, said to Vary According to Race and Sex, with especial reference to the Frontal Lobe. *American Journal of Anatomy*, vol. IX., 1-32, February, 1909.

Owen, R., 1868.—On the Anatomy of Vertebrates, vol. 3, *O.*, pp. 915.

Pearson, H. G., 1904.—The life of John A. Andrew, Governor of Massachusetts, 1861-1865. *O.*, 2 vols. Boston and New York.

Smith, Goldwin, 1892.—The Moral Crusader, William Lloyd Garrison. *D.*, pp. 190, Toronto.

Smith, G. Elliott, 1902.—Descriptions of the Brains of Vertebrates in vol. 2 of the Physiological Catalogue of the Museum of the Royal College of Surgeons of England. 1902.

Spitzka, E. A., 1902.—Contributions to the Encephalic Anatomy of the Races; First paper; Three Eskimo brains. *American Journal of Anatomy*, vol. 2, pp. 25-71.

——1903.—Brain-weights of Animals with special Reference to the Weight of the Brain in the Macaque Monkey. *Jour. of Comp. Neurology*, vol. 13, pp. 9-17, 1903.

——1907.—A Study of the Brains of Six Eminent Scientists and Scholars, etc. *Transactions of the American Philosophical Society*, N. S., vol. 21, part 3. Philadelphia.

Turner, Sir William, 1897.—Some Distinctive Characters of the Human Structure. Address before the Anthropological Section of the British Association for the Advancement of Science. Abstract in *British Medical Journal*, August 21st, 1897, pp. 450-453.

Waldeyer, 1894.—Ueber einige anthropologisch bemerkenswerthe Befunde an Negerhirnen. Berlin Akad. d. Wissenschaften, *Siztungsberichte,* 1894, Band II, pp. 1213-1221.

Wilder, B. G., 1885.—On Two Little-known Cerebral Fissures, with Suggestions as to Fissural and Gyral Names. Amer. Neurol. Asso., *Transactions. Journal of Nervous and Mental Disease,* vol. 12.

——1889.—Article, Brain, Gross or Macroscopic anatomy. Buck's Reference Handbook of the Medical Sciences, vol. 8, pp. 107-164; also vol. 9, pp. 99-110. Second edition, vol. 2, pp. 136-218, 1900.

——1905.—Two examples of the Negro's Courage, Physical and Moral. Address at the Garrison Centenary, Dec. 10, 1905. *Alexander's Magazine,* January and February, 1906. See also the *Sunday News,* Charleston, S. C., Dec. 7, 1902.

——1907.—The Educational Uses of Sharks and Rays, especially the Acanth Shark. Proceedings of the 12th annual meeting of the New York State Science Teachers Association, *Bulletin of the University of the State of New York,* No. 431, 1907, pp. 95-96. (This refers to my previous papers on the same subject.)

Woodworth, B. S., 1909.—Racial Differences in Mental Traits. Address before the Section in Anthropology and Psychology, American Association Adv. Science, 1909. *Science,* February 4, 1910, 171-186.

Work, M. N., 1906.—The Negro Brain. Article 3 of "The Health and Physique of the Negro American." The Atlanta University Publications, No. 11, 1906. Pp. 24-27. W. E. B. DuBois, Editor.

Wyman, Jeffries, 1847.—Osteology of the Gorilla. Part of a paper by Savage and himself. Boston Society of Natural History, *Proceedings,* Aug. 18th. *Boston Journal of Natural History,* vol. 5, part 4, pp. 417-442. [Of this very important memoir some reprints were made for the author in quarto form; for information as to the whereabouts of such the present writer will be grateful.]

——1868.—Observations on Crania. Boston Society of Natural History, *Proceedings,* vol. 11, 1868, pp. 440-462.

——1862.—Account of the dissection of a Hottentot. Boston Society of Natural History, *Proceedings,* April 2, 1862, vol. 9, pp. 56-57; also pp. 352-357, and *Anthropological Review,* III, 330-335.

Address of

Edwin R. A. Seligman

Professor of Political Economy

at

Columbia University

As one of the advocates of that unnatural science of which we have just heard, I desire to say a word only as to the phase of the subject which falls directly within my own sphere, that is, of economics and social science. If there is anything that has been brought out in the papers this morning, I think it is the keen realization of the fact that we must indeed not overlook the forces of heredity or disparage them. After all, the controlling, the really important point to the student of social evolution is the fact of social environment. We may take a leaf out of the book of that great wizard of California, Mr. Burbank, who has shown us how in the course of several generations the character of a plant can be so completely changed that we will have a new genus. Anyone who has given much study to the forces of association, and especially of economic progress, must realize that within a space of a very few generations we find the most profound alterations in what seems to be the very texture of human life.

While I do not wish to range through the whole field of social life, I desire to call attention to the fact that amid all the other important forces at work, the economic consideration is the one which is receiving far more attention to-day than it ever did before. And therein lie the hope and the potency of the future. It is just because the economic environment is changing, just because there is a hope in the future of such fundamental alterations in the environment of the American Negro, that we can look forward with confidence to a point yet to come. At the same time I desire to emphasize in the few words I have to say, one scientific conclusion: the necessity of distinguishing between the individual and the group and the danger of making unduly broad generalizations. What we need above all in social life is to be able to distinguish in our attitude to our fellows, between the individual and the group.

As a member of a race which has also borne hardships, I wish to call attention to this particular fact: It is often said of the Jews that they run through the whole gamut of society; they have both the Jesus type and the Shylock type, coming from one and the same race. Now the trouble with the Negro is that the ordinary man considers only the Shylock type, if there is a man that corresponds to the Shylock type, and that we have not yet learned to appreciate the Jesus type. To me there is nothing more tragic in the whole of human experience than the lot of that American Negro, cultivated, refined gentleman, who at the same time is thrown into the caldron and fused with a mass of his unhappy and more unfortunate brethren. The scientific man, of course, knows no prejudice. I say that, and yet I remember that when I was a student at a German university, shortly after the Franco-Prussian war, there was a strain for some time between the French and the Germans, which shows of course that we are first human and secondly scientific. But at least it may be said that the more scientific we are, the less prejudice we have.

The great advantage of a meeting like this and the great benefit of all knowledge and of all science, is that it tends gradually to enable the ordinary man to distinguish between the individual and the group. That seems to me to be the real hope for the future, because after all, we can expect to see the elevation of the great mass come about only very, very slowly. The great mass of any nation to-day is very little different from the great mass of people thousands and thousands of years ago. It is the great man, it is the sport or freak, of whom the naturalists tell us, who gradually by his own influence, by his own great personality and example, is able slowly to mold and to change these general forces.

As regards the general forces, you must not be misled even if you look at the economic point of view. My own conviction is that things are going to get worse before they get better in this country, so far as the Negro question is concerned, simply because of the exceeding difficulty of bringing to bear the forces of science upon popular imagination. I do not share the pessimistic view, because my view is not pessimistic. But it is nonetheless true that certain economic conditions are now at work in the South which are temporarily going to make things worse. It is because the "poor white trash," as he is called, the ordinary white man, is now coming to his own in the South, that the economic competition and the economic pressure are going to be felt more severely than before. And the hope we have of the future is that slowly and gradually the great men— both the white and the black—that those great men will utilize all the forces of science and all the forces of the higher ethics, and will gradually bring to bear upon this larger mass that environs us all, an appreciation of the more human and the more scientific aspect of the case. Therefore, gentlemen, let us not be mistaken; let us be prepared to face the future as it comes; but let us be prepared also to put up a good fight.

By that I do not mean to say that I have not the utmost sympathy with our friends of the South, both white and black. The human race is about the same all over. We are all, so far as we are not suffused with the scientific instinct, full of prejudice. Put yourselves, the Negro man and woman, into the conditions in which the white man and woman are, and many of you would feel about the whole subject as they do. We have a comparatively easy time in the North. We have not the great temptations to meet. We must not be too harsh in our judgments. But what we must always do is to hold forth and emblazon on our banner the scientific aspect of the question and then there can be only one answer.

That being true, I say there is call for two qualities on the part of the rank and file, as well as among the leaders, of the Negro race—the quality of patience, of recognizing that mankind moves very slowly, and that prejudice gives way to science still more slowly; but on the other hand, the fervent hope and the confident expectation that in the long run, and in the not too long run, the forces of science and the ethical forces, which after all are deep down in the heart of every one of us, white and black—that those forces will continue to grow in their influence and finally achieve their desired and deserved success.

Address of

John Dewey

Professor of Philosophy

Columbia University

The ground has already been so well covered in the matter of this scientific discussion, that I shall detain you but a moment or two, in fact I should not have appeared at all, were it not that it gave me the opportunity to express my sympathy with the purpose of this gathering and to give myself that privilege, I venture to detain you for these very few moments. One point that has been made on the scientific side, might perhaps be emphasized, namely with reference to the doctrine of heredity.

It was for a long time the assumption—an assumption because there was no evidence or consideration of evidence—that acquired characteristics of heredity, in other words capacities which the individual acquired through his home life and training, modified the stock that was handed down. Now the whole tendency of biological science at the present time is to make it reasonably certain that the characteristics which the individual acquired are not transmissible, or if they are transmissible, then in such a small degree as to be comparatively and relatively negligible. At first sight this taken by itself may seem to be a disappointing and discouraging doctrine, that what one individual attains by his own effort and training, does not modify the level from which the next generation then starts. But we have put over against that this other point that has been made with reference to social heredity, and the fact that there is a great difference between mental culture from the standpoint of the individual and mental culture from the standpoint of society.

This doctrine that acquired characteristics are not transmitted becomes a very encouraging doctrine because it means, so far as individuals are concerned, that they have a full, fair and free social opportunity. Each generation biologically commences over again very much on the level of the individuals of the past generation, or a few generations gone by. In other words, there is no "inferior race," and the members of a race so-called should each have the same opportunities of social environment and personality as those of a more favored race. Those individuals start practically to-day, where the members of the more favored race start again as individuals, and if they have more drawbacks to advance, they lie upon the side of their surrounding opportunities, the opportunities in education, not merely of school education but of that education which comes from vocation, from work responsibilities, from industrial and social responsibilities, and so on. It is therefore the responsibility of society as a whole, conceived from a strictly scientific standpoint leaving out all sentimental and all moral considerations— it is the business of society as a whole to-day, to see to it that the environment is provided which will utilize all of the individual capital that is being born into it.

For if these race differences are, as has been pointed out, comparatively slight, individual differences are very great. All points of skill are represented in every race, from the inferior individual to the superior individual, and a society that does not furnish the environment and education and the opportunity of all kinds which will bring out and make effective the superior ability wherever it is born, is not merely doing an injustice to that particular race and to those particular individuals, but it is doing an injustice to itself for it is depriving itself of just that much of social capital.

RACE RECONCILIATION

Celia Parker Woolley

Head-worker Frederick Douglass Centre

Chicago

The color problem does not pertain to this country alone, still less to a particular section of the country. The cry so often heard, "This is a southern problem," "The South alone understands the Negro," "Leave this matter to us" is but a repetition of the old cry which we heard before the war. The same human passion and sectional pride, the same sense of special ownership and right of final appeal inspires the later as the earlier cry. The color question is a national problem, it is a question of republican faith and well-being. Its just settlement is a matter of national honor and moral consistency. If the Negro is a citizen of these United States then his safety and welfare should be as much a matter of patriotic concern in Massachusetts and Illinois as in Mississippi and Alabama. Sectional feeling has no place in the settlement of this problem any more than in questions of the tariff and railway control.

We know what the situation is in India and South Africa, in the Philippines and on the California coast. Everywhere the dark-skinned man is coming to the

74

front, claiming his share in the great comprehensive boon of civilization, with all it holds or implies of material benefit, of individual opportunity, of intellectual gain and social partnership in the common task of building a race that is only incidentally white or black, Oriental or Occidental, Teutonic, Asiatic or Negroid, but first and mainly human. Had we a tithe of the faith and courage which our political and religious professions are supposed to bestow we should recognize in this race or color question but one more demand for those manhood rights which we pretend to grant to all alike, one more application, in a case of special urgency and need which should win instant response, of that religion of reason and righteousness which we profess.

It is not the Negro who is at stake in this controversy, deep and widespread as are his wrongs. It is the white man, the white man's civilization, the white man's republic. It is not a question of Negro supremacy, but of the worth of those claims to superiority which are so easily alarmed for their own safety and continuance. It is not a question of the black man's political enfranchisement, important and just as this phase of the question is. The Negro can better afford to lose his vote than the white man can afford to deprive him of it. The main question underlying this and all our social problems—the woman question, the labor question, and a host of minor problems—is one that casts doubt on all our high professions of democracy and humanity. What is our republic worth? How long and in what fashion will it continue to exist? What is our Christianity worth? Whence do we derive it, from the Sermon on the Mount or from those notions of hierarchy and social separation which the church as an institution condones and fosters?

The present greatest need of the Negro in this country is the discriminating friendship of the white man.

The Negro suffers from a wholesale judgment that makes no distinctions or exceptions. It is only the Negro as cook or butler, waiter or porter, whom the average white man knows and takes into account. What a commentary on our Americanism is that state of mind which decrees an entire class or portion of the state and community to a position of fixed inferiority. The crux of the race question lies not at all in any feeling we may have, favorable or unfavorable, towards the colored cook or butler. It is not the class to which these belong that suffers most from race prejudice, but the colored man and woman who has risen far above the position of menial service, necessary and honorable as this may be. It is the educated man who through hardship and sacrifice, such as in any other case than the American Negro's would have won for him friendly recognition and reward, finds himself in spite of all his efforts still subject to the same popular disfavor, the same restrictions as before.

I do not forget the Negro's share of responsibility for the situation from which he and we suffer. I do not forget the mass of black idleness, ignorance and vice with which the social reformer must deal. The Negro has accomplished marvels for himself in many cases of individual worth and attainment, signalized in names like Washington, Du Bois, Kelly Miller, Scarborough, Kealing, the Grimke brothers, but no one knows so well as these how deep and dire, how constant and pressing are the needs in the lower stratum of Negro life, not in the South alone but in the large cities of the North.

We are in less danger to-day from the crass barbarities of the Tillmans, the Dixons and the Vardamans than from the super-refined and highly intellectualized utterances of certain distinguished scholars. When Senator Tillman accidentally runs across Booker Washington in the White House and, having never before seen the distinguished man of color, improves the occasion to look him over carefully, and says to a waiting reporter afterwards, "He has white blood in him," we only smile with amusement, and comfort ourselves with the reflection that if Mr. Tillman represents the type that is purely white we have reason to be thankful for the mixture of blood currents in the veins of his dark-skinned compatriot.

But when the venerable leader of our most distinguished seat of learning, founded on Pilgrim faith and love of liberty, speaks with unqualified condemnation of race unions of every kind and degree, even between separate families of the same race household, as the English and the Scandinavian, we are in truth grieved and discouraged. But we are at the same time thankful that men like Frederick Douglass and Booker Washington were luckily born and given to the world before the monstrous evil of their mixed race inheritance was discovered.

If race mixture, particularly the mixture of black and white, is of such injurious effect, let us address our arguments and appeals, our warnings and rebukes, to the guilty party—the white man of the South and of the North. Let us attach the crime and the crime's punishment to the sinning factor, and not darken innocent lives and increase ill-doing, punishing the guiltless progeny of such unions. The attitude of the average mind, learned or unlearned, on this phase of the question is as shameless as it is cruel, in its open connivance at crime and social misdoing The majority of people care very little about race mixture so long as it keeps itself safe from polite observation under the dark cloak of illicit practices. It is only when seeking to lift itself from the level of passion and shield itself in honest marriage, graced and upheld by the moralities and amenities of the home, that the sense of moral outrage is aroused. A strange anomaly.

This Race Conference meets at a timely hour and it should be the beginning of a permanent organization, with branches in every large center, whose work is to complete the upbuilding of the republic, to make good our professions of human brotherhood. Its aim must be twofold, to arouse the sense of responsibility among the more privileged and powerful, where social favor and opportunity are found on the white man's side. Its work for the black man is to help and encourage in all ways which conduce to a high and self-respecting, self-sustaining type of manhood.

POLITICS AND INDUSTRY

W. E. B. DuBois

Professor of Economics and History

Atlanta University

Atlanta, Georgia

In discussing Negro suffrage we must remember that in the three hundred years between the settlement of this country and the present, there never has been a time when it was not legal for a Negro to vote in some considerable part of this land. From 1700 to 1909 Negroes have probably cast their ballots at some time in every single state of the Union, and all the time in some states and there has been no period in the history of the land when all Negroes were disfranchised. The early movement for disfranchisement came in two waves: the first, early in the 18th century when Negro freedmen first appeared with required qualifications for voting. In this case Negroes along with Jews and Catholics, were deprived of a vote. This initial movement was persisted in only in South Carolina and Georgia. In all other states, South and North, it subsided and Negroes regularly voted in nearly every other state. Then came a second wave of disfranchisement in the North, about the beginning of the 18th century, which had the same object as the disfranchising clauses in the western states early in the next century: namely, to discourage and drive out free Negroes. The third wave of disfranchisement came in the South about 1830 and marked the end of the abolition movement there, and the beginning of the cotton kingdom. The population of free Negroes began to decrease and the complete subjection of the black race was in sight.

The last wave of disfranchisement began in 1890 in Mississippi and now embraces Virginia, North Carolina and the Gulf states excepting Florida and Texas. These states have adopted four kinds of qualifications: 1. Educational qualifications; 2. Property qualifications; 3. Qualifications of birth; 4. Other miscellaneous qualifications the effect of which depends entirely on local election officials. These qualifications have been proposed with two reasons: (a) To keep the Negroes from voting. (b) To eliminate the ignorant electorate.

Against both these excuses there were strong arguments, but at the time they were gathering force and momentum there came a counter argument that practically stopped all effective opposition to the disfranchisement laws. This argument was that the economic development of the Negro in right lines demanded his exclusion from the right of suffrage at least for the present. This proposition has been insisted on so strenuously and advocated by Negroes of such prominence that it simply took the wind out of the sails of those who had proposed defending his rights, and to-day so deeply has this idea been driven that to most readers' minds the Negroes of the land are divided into two great parties—one asking no political rights but giving all attention to economic growth and the other wanting votes, higher education and all rights. Moreover, the phrase "take the Negro out of politics" has come to be regarded as synonymous with industrial training and property getting by the black men.

I want in this short paper to show that, in my opinion, both these propositions are wrong and mischievous. In the first place there is no such division of opinion among Negroes as is assumed. They are practically a unit in their demand for the ballot. The real difference of opinion comes as to how the ballot is to be gained. One set of opinions favors open, frank agitation. The other favors influence and diplomacy; and the result, curious to say, is that the latter party has to-day an organized political machine which dictates the distribution of offices among black men and sometimes among Southern whites. It is not too much to say that to-day the political power of the black race in America is in certain restricted lines very considerable. But those of us who oppose this party hold that this kind of political development by secrecy and machine methods is both dangerous and unwholesome and is not leading toward real democracy. It may and undoubtedly does put a large number of black men in office and it lessens momentary friction, but it is encouraging a coming economic conflict which will threaten the South and the Negro race.

And this brings me to the second proposition: that political power in the hands of the Negro would hinder economic development. It is untrue that any appreciable number of black men to-day forget or slur over the tremendous importance of economic uplift among Negroes. Every intelligent person knows that the most pressing problem of any people suddenly emancipated from slavery is the problem of regular work and accumulated property. But this problem of work and property is no simple thing—it is complicated of many elements. It is not simply a matter of manual dexterity but includes the spirit and the ideal back of that dexterity.

We who want to build and build firmly the strong foundations of a racial economy believe in vocational training, but we also believe that the vocation of a man in a modern civilized land includes not only the technique of his actual work but intelligent comprehension of his elementary duties as a father, citizen, and maker of public opinion, as a possible voter, a conservor of the public health, an intelligent follower of moral customs, and one who can at least appreciate if not partake something of the higher spiritual life of the world. We do not pretend that all of this can be taught each individual in school but it can be put into his social environment, and the more that environment is curtailed and restricted the more emphatic is the demand that some part at least of the group shall be trained and trained thoroughly in these higher matters of human development, if—and here is the crucial question—if they are going to be able to share the surrounding civilization.

This brings us to the matter of voting. It is possible —easily possible—to train a working class who shall have no right to participate in the government. Most of the manual workers in the history of the world have been so trained. It is also possible, and the modern world thinks desirable, to train a working class who shall also have the right to vote—both these things are possible although the overwhelming trend of modern thought is toward making workers voters. But the one thing that is impossible and proven so again and again is to train two sets of workers side by side in economic competition and make one set voters and deprive the other set of all participation in government. To attempt this is madness. It invites conflict and oppression. A nation cannot exist half slave and half free. Either the slave will rise through blood or the freeman will sink.

So far tremendous effort in the South has been put forth to keep down economic competition between the races by confining the Negroes by law and custom to certain vocations. But, for two reasons, this effort is bound to break down: First there is no caste of ability corresponding with the caste of color, and secondly because if every Negro in the South worked twenty-four hours a day at the kinds of work which are tacitly assigned him, he could not fill the demand for that kind of labor. Economic competition is therefore inevitable as facts like these show: In Alabama there are 94,000 Negro farm laborers and 82,000 whites. In Georgia there are 1,100 Negro barbers and 275 white barbers. In Florida there are 2,100 Negroes employed on railroads and 1,500 whites. In Tennessee there are 1,000 white masons and 1,200 black masons. And so on we might go through endless figures showing that economic competition among whites and blacks was not only existent but growing.

Moreover the schools that increase the competition are the industrial schools and this is both natural and proper. Negro professional men, teachers, physicians and artists come very seldom in competition with the whites. But farmers, masons, painters, carpenters, seamstresses and shoe repairers work at the same work as whites and largely under like conditions. This competition accentuates race prejudice; when a whole community, a whole nation, pours contempt on a fellow-man it seems a personal insult for that man to work beside me or at the same kind of work. Thus one of the first results of the denial of civil rights is industrial jealousy and hatred. Here is a man whom all my companions say is unworthy and dangerous as a companion on the street car or steam car, as a fellow listener at a concert, theatre or lecture, as a table companion in the same house or restaurant, often as a dweller in the same street or same neighborhood and always as a worshipper in the same church or occupant of the same graveyard. If all this is so— and this the Southern white working man is industriously taught from the cradle to the grave—if this is so then why should I be forced to work at the same job as this man or be engaged in similar kinds of work, or receive the same wages? If we cannot play together why should we work together?

Not only is there this feeling but there is also power to act. After the Atlanta riot the police and militia searched the houses of colored people and took away guns and ammunition, while the sheriff almost gave away guns to some of the very men who had composed the mob. We think this monstrous but it is but a parallel of the action of the whole nation: they have put the ballot in the hands of the white workingmen of the South and taken it away from the black fellow-workmen. The result is that the white workman can enforce his feeling of prejudice and repulsion. Other things being equal the employer is forced to discharge the black man and hire the white man—public opinion demands it, the administrators of government, including police, magistrates, etc., render it easier, since by preferring the white many intricate questions of social contact are avoided and political influence is vastly increased.

Under such circumstances there is nothing for the Negro to do but to bribe the employer by underbidding his white fellow: to work not only for less money wages, but for longer hours and under worse conditions. No sooner does he do this than he is mocked at as a "scab" from Mexico to Canada, and visited with all the consequent penalties. He is said to be dragging down labor and he is said to be taking bread from others' mouths and he may be, but his excuse is tremendous: he is dragging others down to keep himself from complete submergence and he is taking some of the bread from others' mouths lest his children starve. Does he *want* to do this? Does he like long hours? Ignorant as he is as a mass, has he not intelligence enough to perceive the value of the labor unions and the meaning of the labor movement? No, it is not because the black man is a fool but because he is a victim that he drags labor down.

Faced by this situation the next step of the white workmen is to enforce by law and administration that which they cannot gain by competition. In the past these laws have been laws to separate and humiliate the blacks, but more aggressive laws are demanded to-day and will be in the future. The Alabama child labor law excepts from its operation children in domestic service and in agriculture—i. e., Negro children. *They* may grow up in absolute ignorance so far as the law is concerned. The Alabama law makes the breaking of a contract to work by a farm laborer a felony punishable by a penitentiary sentence. Such a breaking of law in other industries is a misdemeanor punishable by a fine. Certain oppressive labor regulations in many southern states are only applicable to such counties as vote their enforcement. Counties with white workmen vote it down. Counties with disfranchised black workmen vote it in. In the state civil service no Negro can be employed at any job which any white man wants, for obvious reasons. More than that no white man whose business depends on public approbation, or political concession can dare to hire Negroes or if he hires them promote them as they may deserve. He must often be content with a distinctly inferior grade of white help.

Judges and juries in the South are at the absolute mercy of the white voters. Few ordinary judges would dare oppose the momentary whim of the white mob and practically only now and then will a jury convict a white man for aggression on a Negro. This is true not only in criminal but also in civil suits, so much so that it is a widespread custom among Negroes of property never to take a civil suit to court but to let the white complainant settle it. In all public benefits like schools and parks and gatherings and institutions, Negroes are regularly taxed for what they cannot enjoy. I am taxed for the Carnegie Public Library of Atlanta where I cannot enter to draw my own books. The Negroes of Memphis are taxed for public parks where they cannot sit down.

The public schools of the South on account of virulent opposition of the white working classes are (save in a few cities and a few exceptional counties), worse off than they were twenty years ago—with poorer teachers, lower salaries and more negligent supervisors. This statement covers nine-tenths of the public Negro schools of the South.

Even in serving his own people and organizing his own business the Negro is at the absolute mercy of the white voters. It is often said grandiloquently: let the Negroes organize their own theatres, transport their own passengers, organize their own industrial companies; but such kinds of business are almost absolutely dependent on public license and taxation requirements. A theatre built and equipped could by a single vote be refused a license, a transportation company could get no franchise, and an industrial enterprise could be taxed out of existence. This is not always done, but it is done just as soon as any white man or group of white men begin to feel the competition. Then the voters proceed to put the industrial screws on the disfranchised. Witness the strike of the white locomotive firemen in Georgia today. Negro firemen get from fifty cents to one dollar a day less than the white firemen, have to do menial work and cannot become engineers. They can, however, by good service and behavior be promoted to the best runs by the rule of seniority. Even this the white firemen now object to and say in a manifesto: the "white people of this state refuse to accept Negro equality. This is worse than that." The other day the white automobile drivers of Atlanta made a frantic appeal in the papers for persons to stop hiring black drivers. The black drivers replied, "We have had fewer accidents than you and get less wages," but the whites simply said, "This ought to be a white man's job."

This sort of thing is destined to grow and develop. The fear of Negro competition in all lines is increasing in the South. The demand of to-morrow is going to be increasingly not to protect white people from ignorance and degradation, but from knowledge and efficiency— that is, to so arrange the matter by law and custom as to make it possible for the inefficient and lazy white workman to be able to crush and keep down his black competitor at all hazards, and so that no black man shall be allowed to do his best if his success lifts him to any degree out of the place in which millions of Americans are being taught he ought to stay.

This is bad enough but this is not all. The voteless Negro is a provocation, an invitation to oppression, a plaything for mobs and a bonanza for demagogues. They serve always to distract attention from real issues and to ride fools and rascals into political power. The political campaign in Georgia before the last was avowedly and openly a campaign not against Negro crime and ignorance but against Negro intelligence and property owning and industrial competition as shown by an 83% increase in their property in ten years. It swept the state and if it had not culminated in riot and bloodshed and thus scared capital it would still be triumphant. As it is the end is not yet. The political power of a mass of active working people thus without votes is greater for harm, manipulation and riot than the power of the same people with votes could possibly be, with the additional fact that voters would learn to vote intelligently by voting. Fourteen years ago Mississippi began disfranchising Negroes. You were promised that the result would be to settle the Negro problem. Is it settled? No, and it never will be until you give black men the power to be men, until you give them the power to defend that manhood. When the Negro casts a free and intelligent vote in the South then and not until then will the Negro problem be settled.

RACE PREJUDICE AS VIEWED FROM AN ECONOMIC STANDPOINT

William L. Bulkley

Principal in the Public Schools

New York

I wish to preface my argument with the following indictment: Race-prejudice in the South

(1) Does not recognize the value of an intelligent, contented laboring class. (2) Closes the door to occupations requiring skill and responsibility. (3) Drives out of the South, by humiliating and oppressive laws and practices, many of its most desirable citizens. (4) Forces across the line thousands of mixed bloods. (5) Forces into the ranks of unskilled labor in the North and West many who are skilled.

Considering the race question from a purely economic standpoint, no part of this country, North, South, East or West, ought to continue the unjust industrial restrictions upon us as a people. In the North these restrictions act as an injustice to the weaker race, but do not cause any perceptible economic loss to the community. In the South, on the contrary, any limitation put upon the development of the Negro in any line of manual labor or skill seriously affects its economic development. Already is this loss to its industrial life evident in the desperate efforts exerted to induce European immigration. But the suggestion that this need of more and better labor is caused by her sins of omission or commission would doubtless meet from the South the most robust denials. And yet, any thoughtful student of economics would readily see that this lack of reliable labor is at least in part, due to the absence of effort on the part of the South to enlighten, to encourage and to render contented its laboring classes. With the exception of a makeshift of a school lasting for a few weeks each year, the South offers its farming masses absolutely no other inducement to a larger and better life. Little wonder is it that there are hundreds of thousands of acres cultivated in the same sort of indifferent way year after year.

And again, from the ranks of skilled labor, race oppression is driving out of the South a host of the best Negroes, best in culture of mind, best in sturdiness of character, best in skill of hand. A census of the Negroes in any city in the North would show that the majority of the most progressive of them, whether in the professions, in business, or in the trades, were more or less recent arrivals from the South. Can the South afford to lose this class? Can any country afford to drive out its best? Does not the South need the influence of such men and women over the ignorant, the idle, or the depraved of our race? Is it wise to make living conditions so unbearable that only the most ignorant or the most unworthy are contented to remain and endure with the characteristic grin of a sycophant?

The desirable, the progressive, the intelligent Negroes who remain South are there for one of two reasons: because they can't get away; or because they feel they ought to stay and suffer with their own. And all these heave from the depths of their hearts the despairing cry, "How long, O Lord, how long?"

If only a small part of the time that is devoted to schemes to restrict, to humiliate, and to oppress the Negroes were spent in an effort to study means by which they might be made more intelligent, mort thrifty as laborers, more skillful as artisans, more contented as citizens, there are few spots on the globe that would show so great an industrial awakening during the twentieth century.

Wise legislators in any community would endeavor to enact such laws. or establish such customs as would develop a contented middle and a hopeful laboring class. Indeed, the North and West, with their attractive wages, with their excellent schools, libraries, reading-rooms, clubs, and settlement houses, with a cordial welcome to full American citizenship, have beckoned invitingly the millions of Europeans that make the wealth of these great sections of our nation. During these same years another part of our land has spent its time in devising plans to keep down in dependence and hopelessness its millions of laborers, millions native to the soil, ready and willing to do whatever they are able for the development of the only land they know and the only land they care to know.

In the second place, there is a decided economic loss in keeping within the bounds of unskilled labor those who might do credit in the ranks of skilled labor; and yet that is what the South or any part of the country does when it inhibits and circumscribes the vocations of a part of its people. There are certain classes of skilled labor which it is not permitted a Negro to enter. In fact, my observation convinces me that even certain vocations which belonged almost exclusively to the Negroes ever since the days of slavery are fast being closed against them. The present railroad strike in Georgia illustrates this point. Parenthetically I may say that due credit should be given to the papers, North and South, that have rung out with no uncertain sound about this strike; and yet it would seem impossible to counteract in one day in the year all the evil that these same papers will do us in the other 364 days in written words or insinuations against us as a people. And so down the line there seems to be a purpose to restrict the Negroes within the limits of unskilled labor, to reduce them to a state which, while not nineteenth century slavery may be twentieth century peonage.

Thirdly, as was suggested previously, the humiliating laws and practices are forcing out of the South thousands of its best Negroes, Negroes who love their birthplace, love its balmy air, its sunny skies, its fertile fields, its luxuriant forests, the comradeship of their kith and kin. To us there never cease to come times of yearning to revisit the old spots of our childhood and of our youth, to meet our brethren, to hear their tale of woe, to weep with them over their distresses, to rejoice with them in their successes, to share with them the soul-refreshings that only a Negro revival can give. How near they seem to get to the great loving heart of God in their deep, religious fervor, and childlike trustfulness! But when our yearning seizes us, there appears before us the spectral hand of blighting prejudice, inviting uninvitingly.

I never cease to wonder whether far-sighted white men of the South see the loss in letting so many of their best Negroes leave; whether they ever think that it would be wise to abate their prejudices to the extent of consulting with us for some ground of mutual understanding and sympathy. It is too high a compliment to be credible that we have developed such a large class of desirables that the thousands who leave are easily spared. If a community seeks to acquire and to retain the largest possible number of upright, cultured, property-holding, progressive people, it should inquire into the causes that drive out and keep out this very class. But has there been a single act of a southern Legislature in 35 years aimed to render more comfortable the lot of that class of Negroes who, out of great tribulation, have struggled up and are still struggling up, and rearing their families into clean and commendable manhood and womanhood?

We are needed in the South, needed to help our brethren up, needed to give our white neighbors the assurance of our confidence, needed to join with all honest and earnest men for the regeneration of the land of our birth, scarred by slavery, blighted by the ravages of war, crippled by years of post-bellum misrule, hampered by narrow, near-sighted, selfish prejudice. There is not one of us who would not gladly go back home if we did not know that every right dear to any full man has been ruthlessly torn from our grasp. Gladly would we rush to the embrace of our loved ones in bonds, but we cannot, we cannot.

In the fourth place, we do not get the full economic credit due to us, because of the loss of a host of mixed-bloods who cross the line. Even in the South this crossing occasionally happens. Sometimes the white know it and wink at it, as was evidenced some time ago in the South Carolina State Constitutional Convention in a speech by Mr. Tillman, brother of Senator Tillman. There is scarcely a colored man who could not tell of some friend or relative who has crossed the line North or South, now prominent in business, professors in institutions of learning, married into good society, and rearing families that have no dreams of the depths that their parent has escaped. We could tell the story, if we would —but who would be the knave to disturb their peace?

Lastly, intolerance drives the ambitious, competent, skilled laborer out of the South, but in coming into the North, he meets an industrial competition which he had not figured on. Here he finds the field of skilled labor preempted by the native white man and the foreigner. They guard jealously all approaches to it, whether threatened by Negro or Japanese or Chinaman, or what not. The new arrival attributes to prejudice the difficulties he encounters. I can hardly believe that it is prejudice that keeps Negroes out of the industrial fields in the North as much as other reasons. Only to-day I was talking with a young man, a graduate of Hampton, who has worked his way up to a successful upholstery business in this city. He said, "I had a hard time at first because people didn't believe a colored man could do upholstery work satisfactorily. Now that I have made good, I get plenty of work." I could weary you with numerous instances of this kind.

There are, as I see it, three chief reasons why we are not working easily into the skilled trades in the North: (1) Skepticism as to our ability; (2) The already crowded labor market, that looks with disfavor upon inroads from any source; (3) A feeling, which I think is human, viz., the pleasure found in knocking the weaker fellow. Joseph Bernstein and Max Robinsky would not likely have any feeling against Jim Smith as a man; but as Joseph and Max have just come from a kicking themselves there may be some comfort in finding the chance to try the dose on another fellow. So Pat O'Flannagan does not have the least thing in the world against Jim from Dixie, but it didn't take Pat long after passing the Statue of Liberty to learn that it is popular to give Jim a whack. He would be a little more than human if he did not want to try on Jim what his English lord had so long tried on him. These people who have escaped the persecutions and the class-proscriptions of Europe feel a newly awakened consciousness that they are not after all at the bottom of the heap. They would strike in like manner against any other individual, or religion, or language, or race, provided that they were prompted to it by prevailing custom.

Labor discriminations in the North are not deep-seated and inerradicable. It is impossible to educate the youth of a land in the same schools, in the same classes, side by side in their recitations, united in their sports, shouting the same yell, feeling the same thrill at the success of their colleagues, whether white or yellow or brown or black, without at the same time developing a better understanding with each other, a kindlier feeling toward each other. The thing we call race prejudice in the North differs from race prejudice in the South as a skin-affection differs from scrofula. The latter is organic, in the very blood, drawn in with the mother's milk, and fed by the virus of public sentiment. The other is superficial, readily subject to treatment, and not difficult to cure.

But whatever may be the outcome of the people who leave the South, there is one thing certain—the South is losing a class of citizens which it should wish to retain. Men and women of culture and of character are needed in every community, and in no place more than in the South; but when the Southern whites, by every conceivable means, humiliate, proscribe, and hamper the best of us, there should be no surprise if we seek more congenial climes, where we can at least protect our wives and daughters from the contumely that the lowest white man can heap upon them with absolute impunity.

Whither are we tending? Are we drifting with a sort of fatalistic indifference? Or is there a purpose behind all these restrictions, all these proscriptions?

If there be a purpose what can it be? Is the purpose to go back to slavery? I had hoped that it had been settled, forever settled, that this country cannot exist part slave and part free. If there be no purpose behind it all, there is lacking that far-seeing statesmanship which every government should have. It is difficult to believe that the problem of ten million citizen-aliens does not merit the wisest statesmanship. We are forty-six years from the Emancipation Proclamation, and yet to-day so widespread is this race-oppression that a gathering of this kind is imperative. At the same rate of retrogression, in forty-six more years the then twenty millions of colored people will be veritable serfs.

What would that mean to the country at large? A tuberculous bacillus from a black man's lung is as contagious as a bacillus from a white man's lung. Black men of vicious lives cannot fail to affect to a greater or less degree the communities where they live. You cannot circumscribe vice; it is contagious. Leave these millions of Negroes to battle alone with this terrible weight with which they are now burdened and they would prove themselves little better than mortals if they did not follow the lines of least resistance and sink lower and lower into indolence, vagrancy and criminality. You may deprive a man of the right to vote, but you cannot deprive him of the right to steal.

Give them encouragement. Offer them incentives for intelligence, for skill, for sobriety, for character. Let them feel that as they push themselves out of the quagmire, they will be recognized on their merits. Reward industry. Recognize proved ability. But, if for the sake of argument, it be granted that they are all that their most virulent enemies charge them with being, so much greater is the need of sparing no efforts for their uplift, not so much for their sakes as for your sakes. If it were only one man or a hundred men, there might be some hope of their dying or some way might be suggested to get rid of them; but here is a race of 10,000,-000, as many people as are in all British America and all Central America; they are not dying out; they are not going to die out. As I see it there are only four things possible: (1) Expatriate them; (2) Annihilate them; (3) Degrade them; (4) Elevate them. If they remain here and are allowed no incentives to pull upward, it must follow as the night the day, they will surely run downward.

To work in any way that one has the ability should be the inalienable right of every American citizen. A clean, attractive, honest-looking young man came to my office last week to see if I could help him. He stated that he is a Junior in the pharmaceutical course at Columbia. He desires to spend his vacation in a wholesale drug concern for the sake of needed information and experience. He had written to several drug establishments in this city. He received replies to call, intimating that there were opportunities for work. He stated that he had just come from a useless round of visits to the stores, for the proprietors had suddenly changed their minds on seeing him. Now, that young man is good enough to sit by the side of and work with the best in Columbia University; is it not presumable that he is good enough to work out in the world .by the side of those who are no better than his mates in college?

We do not ask for charity; all we ask is opportunity. We do not beg for alms; we beg only for a chance. The right to work; opportunity to work; encouragement to work; reward for work; this is all we ask; less than this should not be given.

THE NEGRO AND THE SOUTH
William English Walling
Secretary of the Committee

The chief object of any movement in behalf of the American Negro must be to enlighten the public opinion of the whole country. In no section is it in a satisfactory state. Yet in the East, West, and North, the Negro has friends in every social class, sometimes many, sometimes few, who are ready to treat him in every way as on his individual merits. As a southerner born, and one familiar with the southern view through family and friends, from infancy, I am peculiarly conscious that it is in the South alone that the Negro *seems* to find no true brotherly feeling in any element of the white community. It is my chief purpose to point out that the situation is not so bad as it appears, but the fact that the sentiment friendly to the Negro in the South receives at the present moment no effective public expression. That it is disorganized, that it is only locally known in the South and never reaches the North is only too obvious. I shall also admit that this new friendliness is only slightly developed and only half-conscious, that it must oppose at every point the dominant note of prejudice and oppression that pervades and dominates the press, the politics, the pulpit, and even the universities of that section. But whether developed or not, whether discouraging or the reverse, whether we like it or not, it is southern opinion that must ultimately play the chief part in the settlement of this question.

Now what is the present state of opinion in the southern states? To give an intelligent answer we must adopt a new method, we must speak separately of the various elements of the community. Doubtless there seems to be a solid South and there is some truth in the expression, perhaps more than there would have been a generation or two or three generations ago. Yet chemical substances and biological organisms were never understood until they were pulled to pieces, analyzed in every conceivable manner, and we shall not know anything whatever of southern opinion as long as we think of a solid South. The South never was solid. Economic conditions may have produced a tendency towards solidification for the first half of the last century and political sectionalism both North and South may have strengthened this tendency for another fifty years, but the differences within the South on this question during all this period remained, and still remain, infinitely more important and instructive than the points on which unity seemed to prevail. Within the last two decades, moreover, political and economic sectionalism are both decreasing, the same economic questions are dividing the South as divide the rest of the country, each of the new economic or political groups that results takes a new attitude on the Negro problem.

Hitherto the Negroes themselves and their northern friends have placed altogether too much hope in the more cultivated and benevolent of the southern aristocracy, the descendants largely of the wealthier and more humane slave owners of the past generation. But even when such individuals succeed in freeing themselves entirely from local tradition and interests, which happens but rarely, even when they have the tremendous courage to speak out against the overwhelming power of the firmly seated oligarchies that govern the southern states, they represent only isolated individual opinions. Indeed, all the humanitarian opinion of the country combined with that of science could have little effect.

We have been taunted by the fact that we have only three white southerners on our programme. Such criticism ignores the fact that none can speak with such knowledge and even breadth on the condition of the Negroes as some of the enlightened colored southerners we have with us. But it ignores further the very crux of the whole problem, that liberal southerners have given up in despair before the wave of aggressive and ugly reaction that rules the section.

A gentleman from the far South who has written that the racial discrimination had no other basis than the desire to establish by law and custom a legally inferior caste in the place of slavery has written us the reasons why he does not consider it admissible for him to address this conference. Referring to his published writing he says: "I wrote for the country at large to repel false statements which are constantly being made concerning our Negro population, and which, I felt, were doing much to make the Negro obnoxious to those who would naturally be his friends." But he refuses to repeat this denunciation of false statements because he does not feel that most southerners are open to the truth. He writes further, "Should I give utterance anywhere in the North to what I think about the race question, I feel that I should convince nobody in the South that I was right." He then shows the hopeless isolation even of moderate liberals like himself in the South in the statement "there are doubtless other southern men who think as you and I do, but they are certainly not many enough to escape the epithets, crank and fanatic."

What could be more ill-founded and misleading then than the view so widely held in the North and just expressed by President Taft at Howard University, that "the white men of progress were coming to appreciate the advantage of having a class like the colored men that they have there." The slave-owners and all their successors who have secured any *advantage* from having the Negroes there have always appreciated their presence—only the poorer whites have complained of the competition of their cheap labor and wished them in Liberia. It is made a crime in some southern states to entice the colored laborer out of the state even for his benefit. The Negro is recognized as highly valuable, but not as having any rights.

In other words, there are two Souths, those who employ Negro labor and those who compete with it. Those who employ want their labor to be cheap and skilled. To keep it cheap, they hold all the positions of power in the community and in agricultural sections make striking a crime, while they discourage the higher education necessary to produce Negro leaders and drive the most courageous and intelligent to the North. To make it skilled they encourage industrial education. Those who compete with Negro labor cannot wish it to be cheap. One recourse is to keep it unskilled, to exclude it from the unions, but another way is to make common cause in the organized fight for higher wages. Both courses are being followed, and it is right here where the influence of a powerful public sentiment could best aid the Negroes. The white workingmen must be persuaded that their only permanent welfare is co-operation with their colored fellow-workers and that opposition must inevitably lead to total demoralization of all organized effort of both classes.

What is still more interesting is that these two economic Souths coincide to a very large extent with the two geographical Souths. In the Black Belt in the far southern states, South Carolina, Georgia, Alabama, Mississippi, Louisiana and Florida, the employers, especially of the large plantations, have no choice but to employ

Negro labor. They are therefore influenced exclusively by the desire for labor both cheap and as skilled as it may be without becoming discontented. On the other hand, the employers and manufacturers of North Carolina, Virginia, West Virginia, Maryland, Kentucky, Tennessee and Missouri employ more white than colored labor and recognize that it is impossible to legislate against white labor, and, therefore, very difficult to legislate against the colored. On the other hand, it is in these border states exclusively where the competition between colored and white labor assumes very important proportions. In those counties where the prejudice is most strong as well as in the corresponding counties north of the Ohio there are frequent efforts to drive the Negroes out. On the other hand, many of the trade unions make a serious and often successful effort to organize.

In other words, employing whites absolutely dominate the far South, whereas employed whites have a considerable voice in the government of the border states. Geographically as well as economically there are two Souths. In the first, undeveloped workers are held in slavery while the most developed are expelled. In the second, the most developed may often be welcomed while the undeveloped or half-skilled are likely to be expelled. It is from the first South that the leaders of southern opinion are for the most part developed. It is they, at any rate, almost exclusively the descendants of slave-owners, that set the whole tone of public opinion of the whole section. This is why it is almost impossible that a truly friendly sentiment should be developed in the South among the so-called better element. Not among the so-called better element, the class that refers to itself in the South as the aristocary, is the Negro to expect his friends, but from the despised "poor whites." It is upon these that the burden of competition with cheap Negro labor chiefly falls, and it is they that are most sorely tempted by demagogues like Governor Hoke Smith of Georgia to steal the Negro's job. Governor Smith said in 1907 that he stood for the elimination of all competition between blacks and whites, and he has shown a dozen times during the recent strike that he is using his power as governor to this end. He favors for the Negro the "natural status of his race, that of inferiority." Why should we be surprised, then, if a union asserts that the "South is a white man's country," and that therefore no Negro is to be placed above any white?

But this is not what the ex-slave-owners or "those who appreciate the advantage of having the colored men there" mean by a white man's country. They mean that the white man is to have the Negro do his work on his own terms. The white laborer at his worst wants the Negro's job. He has nothing to gain and everything to lose by the establishment of any form of industrial slavery whether first applied exclusively to Negroes or not.

The white laborer's race antagonism has an easy remedy. When there are plenty of jobs he works gladly beside the Negro and admits him in his union. Only when jobs are scarce is he tempted to take advantage of the protection of local governments to drive the Negroes from their jobs or in some border districts, North and South, to drive him from town.

In industries where the Negroes are numerous, the whites necessarily organized in the same unions have no notion of demanding preferential treatment. On the contrary, they fight with the Negroes against those very oligarchies that maintain themselves solely by anti-Negro agitation. Mr. Fairley, head of the United Mine Workers for the Alabama district, has written the conference, "I may say that the treatment accorded to the southern working white man by the southern oligarchy is little if any better than accorded to the Negro, and therefore I agree with you that the interest of the Negro and white laboring man are inseparably one. The action of the state government in our recent strike last summer in Alabama proved that beyond the possibility of a doubt."

The effort of the laboring people to organize and fight collectively for better wages and better conditions, has in fact met with measures of coercion such as have prevailed in no other part of the country unless we except some of the Rocky Mountain states. Leaders of powerful labor unions which have branches in the South are agreed that the southern white laborer can scarcely expect greater justice from the present state governments than the Negro himself. A very important union official (whose name I am not able to disclose), a man widely respected through the country, was ordered to leave the state by one of the governors of a large southern commonwealth.

If justice is to be done to the Negro in this democratic country, it must be done through the enlightened and active interest of some important element or elements of the population. Already a certain part of the people of the South have learned that the disfranchisement and civil discriminations must necessarily affect at the same time the poorer elements of the white population. This has happened largely as follows: Economically considered, the Negroes constitute (with important exceptions), the lowest third of the population, the poor whites the middle third, and the descendants of the former slave-owning aristocracy and gentry and their direct dependents, together with the well-to-do classes with which they are politically allied, the third on top. When the Negroes or a large part of them, were allowed to vote, the "poor whites" held the balance of power, and it was through this balance of power that the Populists at one time obtained such a wide hold on this section and that such men as Governor Varda-man of Mississippi were able to overthrow the old aris-tocracy. Now that the overwhelming part of the Ne-groes are prevented from voting (by legal or illegal means), the poorer whites are forced to share their power with their former rivals, or rather, the political power has passed into the hands of a social group plac-ed somewhere between the poorer whites, properly speaking, and the so-called aristocracy.

As a result of this loss of political power by the "poor whites" we see in various parts of the South the economic system of peonage and the political system of government by terror, invented originally for use against the Negroes turned against certain elements of the white population, especially foreigners. It was even proposed recently in certain Mississippi towns to segre-gate the Italians in the public schools. In Biloxi, Mis-sissippi, the disregard for the propertyless classes has gone so far that an effort has been made recently to force those who could not pay their municipal taxes to work on the streets. Innumerable examples of a grow-ing despotism can be collected from all the southern states. Let us mention only the convict labor system applied in some places to whites as well as blacks, by which a shortage of labor is supplied by the loan of prisoners, and judges friendly to employers are placed under the temptation of increasing this supply.

All this in the far South. As is well known, all of the border states have been more or less evenly divided politically for many years and among these states we may soon be able to include both North Carolina and Tennessee. This condition of comparative political health has already led to a very rapid and most encour-aging increase of true democracy in government, and there is every reason for belief that if the other sec-tions of the country took a stand for the Negro's rights

at the same time that they assumed a friendly attitude
to the true democracy of the South and ceased to view
the Negro situation as a sectional question, all the border states would begin to assume a fairer attitude towards the persecuted race.

This leaves only to be considered the eight states of
the far South and Virginia. As we have pointed out
the white laboring element of the section is already wav-
ering. Only twelve or fourteen years ago a large element of the white farming population in several states
was co-operating with a similar Negro element. The
object of any promising movement, first, last, and all
the time, must be to find in behalf of the Negro means
to encourage these small beginnings of the feeling of
friendliness.

With these facts and this possibility in view, why
can we not hope that a few years of the right policy
may secure an increasing measure of justice for the
Negro in the border states and that a generation of national co-operation and education, national organizations
of farmers and workingmen, may even convert the
white masses of the far South to a correct attitude?
The more numerous elements of the population are
those who will finally decide, and they are almost certain to decide justly since it is precisely these poor farmers and laboring people that are economically most
nearly related to the Negro.

This policy does not imply that an appeal should not
be made at the same time to the descendants of slave-
owners, in their own interests and those of the South,
as well as in the interest of justice and humanity; nor
on the other hand that the rest of the nation should re-
lent in any way its demand for the enforcement of the
Fourteenth and Fifteenth Amendments, for they bring
to bear that very form of pressure, just and gentle, that
conscience does not allow us to dispense with, and that

is the only way one brother may really hope to prevent even the worst errors of another. But as long as the solid South resists we can hardly expect a very thorough enforcement. To accomplish this, we must first break the solid South. The effort that has been made in the name of imperialism and a prohibitive tariff must be made in the name of democracy.

The masses of the southern population must be shown that their interests lie in a gradual extension of the suffrage to the Negroes as fast at least as the latter can receive a moderate school education. They must realize that it is to their interest to provide for this education as rapidly as possible, and in spite of their poverty they must show the widest liberality in this respect. The northern democracy, on the other hand, would be tremendously strengthened, if Senators Tillman and Bailey and their like were replaced in the national councils by true Democrats representing the educated white laborers and farmers as well as the educated Negroes of those or other economic classes. Such an accession to the national legislature would immensely strengthen the popular cause throughout the whole nation. In return, a body of true southern representatives could demand effectually from the nation a fair treatment not only for the southern farmers and workingmen but of the whole South a fairer treatment than has ever been received or ever could be through any alliance based upon any other principle than that of democracy itself.

As some Negroes have expressed it, it is now proposed by certain parties, to cement the friendship of the whites of the North with the whites of the South over the prostrate body of the Negro. On the contrary, it is to the direct economic and political interest of the true southern democracy, whether white or colored, whether of the Republican or Democratic parties, to join hands with the corresponding democracy of the North. Imperialism or the cause of a prohibitive tariff could unite only certain restricted elements of the two sections, however powerful socially and economically these elements may be. Only by the nationalization of our existing democracy, by its extension into the South through the better organization and representation of the masses of the southern people, can sectionalism be eliminated. Any other method must first leave the masses of the country divided on geographical lines as before, and then by forcing the Negro backward, endanger the very foundation of their power. For if the class that rules the South at the present moment, with its anti-Negro propaganda, once succeeds in making a permanent alliance with the corrupt corporations and politicians of the North, now fortunately segregated in another party, a far more dangerous system of class rule will be evolved in America than we had before the Civil War; and this unholy alliance is impending this very moment. The class that stands for persecution of the Negro once given a share in our national government will stand for any and every other form of attack on free and democratic institutions, every form of reaction known to eastern Europe.

No greater peril stands before democrats of every race in this country than the permanent participation of the southern reactionary element in our national legislature, no greater hope than that the true democracy of the South shall be properly presented in our national counsels, no matter through what party. The Negro's only hope is at the same time the sole safeguard of the nation. This is the thought and the hope of the farmers and workingmen of the whole nation to their southern brethren: By lowering the political and economic status of the colored population which furnishes half your co-workers in agriculture and industry, you inevitably cut in half your own ability to resist greedy employers, or those economic forces against which farmers have to contend. You gain nothing from cheapened labor in the towns and cheapened prices on the farms that inevitably result from the crushing of the colored population. Many of you have already learned what you suffer at the hands of the present oligarchies and have frequently found yourselves forced to unite with the Negroes against them. Now join yourselves once for all with us your brother farmers and workingmen from other sections of the country. Do not allow yourselves to be longer divided from us by the false fear of Negro domination. By so doing you not only rivet your own chains but you hold back the whole country. Join us, bring with you the best elements of the colored population, whose aid you will find indispensable for your own emancipation in the South, and we will see to it that your interests and welfare are advanced in the national government as never before for a hundred years.

Remain divided from us and we are helpless to aid you or protect ourselves. Join us and victory of the cause of progress and democracy is assured.

DISCUSSION

MR. WALDRON: There are many things that I would like to say, but I want to emphasize that I believe we have not laid enough stress on the white side of this thing. The Negro side is bad, but unless something is done to change things, the poor white man not only of the South, but particularly in the South, is going to feel the pinch of the shoe just as much as the Negro.

MR. BANNON: We are very much encouraged that we are permitted to have the privilege and opportunity of meeting with white men and white women and converse about these matters. I think my Negro friends, that if the Negro will show a little more spirit, and stand up on his feet, the white man will stand by him.

MR. STEMMONS: The man must be dull indeed who does not realize the crisis reached in the race situation in this country. I believe that no better opportunity has ever been presented and that no better ever will be presented again for starting the flood of influence which controls the situation flowing in the right direction. But let us not be deceived. Unless we meet this situation with dignity, wisdom and foresight, we will merely add fuel to flames already raging in this country, and make it more difficult than ever before to overcome the same. Everybody in this presence very likely has the same idea of the race situation in this country. For a few individuals to hold an ideal, to create an ideal which they are willing to live up to, and which they believe the general public ought to live up to, is a noble thing; but for them to produce a line of action that will override opposition and make this ideal part of the public life, is quite another thing. If mere conferences and talks and resolutions and protests and appeals were all that are needed, we have already enough of these to settle a dozen such questions instead of making it worse and worse, as has been the case with the race situation in this country for the past forty-five years. The trouble has been, I think, our failure to recognize and act upon the influences that control this situation and keep it alive, failure to recognize and appreciate the basic conditions upon which depend the development of the race.

Give us an economic opportunity, that is what the race asks. The physical conditions of the race depend upon it. For example, a good many people say to me that the conditions of the Negro are gradually improving throughout the country. Ask them for their basis for such an assertion, and they say the colored people are owning better houses, building bigger churches, engaging in more businesses and in more diversified branches of labor than ever before. We admit this, but I refuse to admit it without ample qualifications.

I refuse to accept that point, because while a few Negroes are successful in this way, in business and in professional lines, at least eighty per cent. of the colored people are engaged in domestic and personal labors, and the lines against them in these avenues of labor are being drawn closer and closer each succeeding year. Why, the most important field that we have had in the North for colored men has been working at the hotels. But now, with very few exceptions, none of the first-class hotels will employ a colored waiter. There is not a first-class hotel in any northern city that will employ colored men. Furthermore, on the menus of these hotels you will find a statement: "Nothing but white help employed in this establishment." Ten years ago in reading in the help wanted columns of any daily newspaper, you would find a large percentage of domestic situations specifying Negroes. To-day there are comparatively no calls for a Negro domestic, while an increasing percentage of the calls for domestics specify that none but white are needed.

But notwithstanding the extent to which they are being excluded along lines of these domestic and personal services, we all know that it is almost impossible for them to find lucrative employment in any other line. I say, and I challenge anyone to refute my contention, that the opportunities of the colored people are growing fewer and fewer throughout all parts of this country. And I believe there is not another race of people who will so placidly and indifferently permit themselves to be pushed aside in the industrial enterprises of this country, as will the Negro.

MR. STEMMONS: Did you ever sit down and seriously ask yourself the question, why the colored people stay in the South and submit to the indignities and insults heaped upon them? I will tell you why. It is because of their knowledge that they cannot make an honest living in any other part of the country. That is the sum and substance of the matter, to make it possible for the Negroes to live in the South, to so adjust and regulate industrial opportunities throughout the country that no man more than any other may have an advantage.

MR. J. MORGAN, of Brooklyn: The question is simply one of bread and butter. If there be not sufficient bread and butter to go around, the white man certainly has every reason to think that he has a right to attack the Negro as he has attacked him to-day.

The problem confronting us to-day is simply that the Negro is placed in a position where he is losing his political rights. As Professor DuBois has well said, as he loses his political rights, he naturally loses those economic rights that he is heir to. He is just as much an heir to his economic rights, I say, as the whitest man or the blackest man is heir to Milton, or is heir to Galileo, or whatever the world has done; to all these the Negro is just as much heir as any other member of you here.

Mr. WILLIAM M. TROTTER, of Boston: The existence of color lines in industrial matters is calamitous— the industrial and civil differentiation of political matters, as has been so well described to-day. But to my mind that which is the grossest calamity and the most telling, and I must say the grossest outrage, seems to me the attitude of the federal government, which is guilty of standing in the position of giving its authority to color proscription. Now, I think the strike in Georgia has opened our eyes. It has been the boast of the South that while they have denied the colored man political rights, they give him industrial freedom and liberty. And what do we find? We find that in the South the right of the colored man to work is being denied. When they can do it, they can turn a colored man out of any line of work for which they can secure a white. And why is this? Because he is disfranchised. We know that Congress refused to take hold of this political situation, either to stop this disfranchisement or punish it, although in the Fourteenth and Fifteenth Amendments Congress specifically has this power, and it is its duty to do so. We know the Supreme Court dodges the issue, and when it is finally face to face with it, asserts that it is not for the Supreme Court, it is for Congress. And with reference to the declaration of the President of the United States, I think that is most serious. I have read and re-read it, and it seems to me that it is the most insidious and skilful, and therefore the most dangerous attitude ever taken by a President. He admits that a man is not disfranchised on account of color, and he calls that a step in the right direction. Now he goes on to discuss these revised statutes under which he admits we have a franchise, and finally he comes down to a statement something like this: That as long as these laws stand, it is neither the disposition nor is it within the province of the federal government to interfere with the southern states in the handling of their domestic affairs.

Now, my friends, that reads to me like a justification of colored disfranchisement. As a matter of fact, it is. And I have come to this conference to say that we have to face the facts that are before us, and the conditions that are before us, no matter in how high places. Someone has said here that we have too much agitation; that what we want is to get industrial opportunity. We do want to get industrial opportunity, but if we are not to have our franchise, it certainly has been shown that we will lose industrial opportunity. Mr. Taft goes one step further. He says something which it seems to me absolutely indefensible, and which is in line with our talk. He has announced, and you all know it, that colored men should be given office by the colored people, not as a right of citizenship, and that the government should see to it whether or not the appointment is going to help the race. Now, my friends, if the President of the United States is going to openly announce as President of this country, that the colored citizens or the white citizens are to be consulted about the positions to be held by colored men, you have the authority and seal of our highest official behind the idea that the colored people cannot hold positions that other people do not want them to have, because it will do the colored people more harm than good.

Mr. Charles Edward Russell: I don't believe myself, as a matter of fact, that we are going to help the situation very much by moving our colored brethren from the South to the North, or from the North to the South. I don't believe it is going to help very much to assist him if he is a good workman; but I do believe that the remedy, if you want one, lies only in an appeal to the innate conscience of the American people. I can't think that we have had too much agitation. I can't think that we have had enough agitation. I have been following my colored brother with my sympathy, with all my heart, because my father was an abolitionist, and I am bound to say that I have had more education on this question since ten o'clock this morning, than I have had before in all the rest of my life, and I think I have been a pretty close observer. I can tell you that what I have heard to-day has opened up an entirely new horizon to me. And I say this although I am a student more or less and in a position where I can see the world as it goes by. Now there are only a few of us here, but it is a beginning, and everything has to have its beginning, every great movement has to have its beginning, and if we will strike hands together and increase our numbers and look forward, we will have our remedy, if we faint not, believe me.

MR. BARBER: It is because I wish to go on record, as regards the question which has been raised by one of my friends here, that I am so anxious to speak. I want to say that there is a great fundamental difficulty at the bottom of this problem, and it lies not in economics but in politics. On that question I am with William Lloyd Garrison, Mr. Russell, and the other men that have taken the stand here. If you will give a man the right to vote, if you will put the ballot in his hands, if you will give him the right to protect himself, and if he will see that the proper man goes to Congress, a man who will see that American citizens are protected in their rights, then you will get these other things. If you want to solve the race problem, you have to get men who have the right to vote, to say who shall be the governor or the judge, with the right to sit on juries to protect themselves, the right to punish sheriffs for doing what they have done in office. And when you come to this place and tell me that economics and industry are going to solve this problem, I think you are radically wrong. Industry should be just merely a stepping stone to higher things in this republic, and I wish to say the thing that is needed more particularly in this problem is more backbone. If you are going to solve the race problem, you must have men of the William Lloyd Garrison stripe. You must have men that will be willing to stand up for humanity, and for their convictions on this question.

Mr. Benson: I did not expect to have anything to say until some one spoke about moving the Negroes from the South to the North. I believe that if we are going to settle this problem that it is the white who must settle it, and not the other, and I hope that whatever methods are determined upon by this conference, they will be planned upon methods that are natural to us—natural to us in the South, and natural to us in the North. I am only going to speak for one particular section of the country, and that is the South, and I am only going to speak for one particular section of the South, and that is the rural district, because that is where my experience has been, and I don't know very much about anything else. What are we going to do to keep the Negroes from going to the north? It is to make labor remunerative so that he can exist in the South.

I was born and reared in a little rural community in Alabama to which I returned after graduating from college, and to which I have devoted my life, and I want to say that there is probably not a community in the South where the relations between the two races have been so pleasant, and where the people are so well satisfied as they are there. Why? Because they have something to do, and you can't ride through that community and look at the schools and tell which is the white man's school, or which is the black man's school. I only mention this to tell you that we are not dissatisfied down there. We will welcome all that you can do for us in the way of bringing us our rights to vote, but we can't sit down and argue while you are bringing us this right. And the most healthful thing that we all can do, is to bring into the communities those influences which are going not only to help to make a revenue, but are going to help make life as pleasant and attractive there as any other place in the world.

MR. MILLER: We are fully convinced, from the address delivered by Mr. DuBois this afternoon, that the millennium has not come as yet. But in seeking the solution of these questions we are confronted by the question as to whether Mr. Barber is correct in saying that it is not an economic, but a political point of view. Well, it depends largely upon the point of view. I think economics is at the foundation of the whole thing. But we must come to economics through politics, so it depends upon the viewpoint largely as to the truth of the whole thing. I have studied the colored man pretty well, and I find the greatest difficulty with the colored man as a rule is that he is true to one thing. I don't find him ordinarily true to his religion, I don't find him true to his friends, I don't find him true to his trusts. He is just as derelict in these things as the white man. But I find the one thing that the colored man is devoted to, and that ideal is Republicanism. That is his religion. Now it is not until a colored man can break away from this ideal, this religion of Republicanism, that he will get his liberty through economics. Of course Mr. Taft, or Mr. anybody else, can treat the colored man as Mr. Taft treats him, and the colored man can be treated as the Supreme Court treats him, he can be treated as Congress treats him, as long as this colored man will stand firmly by the Republican ticket. We know that in various parts of the country they rebel, they say we will cut the party, we will organize an independent party, or we will stand by some other old party, but on the eve of election day, the great majority of them will come together and say, let us trust the dear old party one more time—and the Republicans know it. Now, there is the great Socialistic party which stands for economic independence, which is the hope of the future to-day. I stand for rights. There are some people who say they want certain rights and do not want others. Some people say they are not looking for social equality. I want every kind of equality I can have. By that I do not mean that I want to force myself upon any man's presence. I never sought a man socially in my life, and I don't expect to. I don't care whether he be rich as Carnegie, holy as St. John, wise as Socrates, or white as the Albanian fathers, but what I want is equality, and if I don't get equality, then I want superiority. Under Socialism we have economic independence. Everyone has the right to work and every man has the full reward of his labors.

Mrs. Ida Wells Barnett: I think perhaps I ought to say something regarding what has been said about agitation, about the beginnings of things, about the small things. Our people of course cannot very clearly see these things from the scientific standpoint, they have not the training necessary to see abstract things as clearly as they see the concrete. To them, therefore, as has been said here this afternoon, this question of talking seems to be a rather small thing, and it is in a way. There is a kind of talking that does not accomplish anything, and there is a sort of talking that does, that makes for the beginning of great things. I have had in mind something which might be called recrimination and we will not hold ourselves blameless in all these matters of which we speak. I want to say as a last word to my own fellow-citizens of the darker side of this house: Let us ask ourselves first if we ourselves have done all that we should do in helping to bring about the things so necessary, and in helping others. Fifteen years ago when the agitation was begun in this country, or launched in England and afterwards in this country, and the question of funds arose with which to do the work of spreading information regarding lynching, a plea was sent out from the Atlantic to the Pacific to get contributions of nickels and pennies and dimes for our own people. That was the beginning of things to show the American white people that they did not know the facts. It was your duty and it was my duty to tell them these facts, to put them in their minds and to read them to them. Did we do it? How much money did we give? How much more did we tax ourselves in order that we might help in bringing about this work? Now don't let us discourage these friends that have come to help us. Let us not spend the time talking about who is to blame on the other side of the line, but let us close up our lines, and not forget that this is only the beginning of the thing. Let us prepare to spread the information in order to get these other people interested in the matter and we will find that with their help we will be able to go forward.

MR. TRIDON : What we white people need is education. I am sick of hearing white people talk about educating the Negro. I am sick of hearing about uplifting men. It seems to me when a man needs to be uplifted, he is not worth bothering about. But you need to get the white people. You need to show that you are not beasts. The white people think you are beasts. They know it. They learned it in school. The boys should not doubt the words of their teachers. Why should those white people doubt the words of their teacher?

But they will if you give them proofs to the contrary. If you will distribute pamphlets and literature; if you will blow your own horn you will get your audience. We must find books and pamphlets published by the colored man, and we must have some kind of a publication which at least shall show not only when a colored man assaults a white woman, but when a colored man saves the life of a white woman.

MR. ROBINSON: A remedy has been asked for, and I would suggest that the remedy used by William Lloyd Garrison is a very good one. It is a very slow but a very effective one. When Mr. Garrison first began his addresses against slavery, he could not get a room in a house in Boston, and he had to give his first talks on the streets. It seems to me that we never bring about any desired results without a little time. It takes time to make men competent. Our best workmen are those who have suffered, who have been the men who worked the hardest and who became competent very slowly, and many of them not at all. I was born and brought up in Louisiana, in the rural districts, and I worked for five or six years for a farmer. One day I said to him, "Captain, what do you think of the so-called race problem? I see it in all the papers. What do you think of it?" He said, "I don't think there is any race problem. You are working for me, do I give myself any concern about your work?" I said, "You don't." He said, "It is the same thing with regard to your race. I give myself no concern with regard to your race. You are solving your own problem, aren't you?" and I said, "I am"; and he said, "That is just how it will be with your race." And I said, "I believe you."

Address of

Judge Wendell P. Stafford

of the

Supreme Court of the District of Columbia

I believe in the fatherhood of God and the brotherhood of man. Not the brotherhood of white men but the brotherhood of all men. I believe in the golden rule and the Declaration of Independence, and I stand by the Constitution of the United States, including the Fourteenth and Fifteenth Amendments. That is my creed and my platform.

Some questions are difficult because they are so complicated. Others are difficult because they are so simple. Duty is apt to be difficult, and the simplest duty may yet be the hardest. I assume that human nature is substantially the same in every climate and under every skin. I assume that the white people of the South are in themselves no better and no worse that the white people of the North. I assume that their opinions and conduct are what ours might have been if we had come under the same influences and conditions. But such considerations do not settle the question: what is right?

The broad subject of our conference is the Negro and the nation, not the Negro and the North, not the Negro and the South, not the Negro and the white man, but the Negro and the nation. The questions it brings up are national. They cannot be settled by any one race and still less by any one section. They concern the whole country and they must be answered by the country as a whole. If the Constitution is not binding in South Carolina it is not binding in New York. If it cannot protect the black man it cannot long protect the white. If fifteen states can set aside the Constitution at their pleasure there is no Constitution worth the name. If a state can nullify one clause it can nullify the whole. If a state can, in a single congressional district, deliberately exclude three-fourths of its eligible voters from the polls on the real ground of color, and yet insist upon having them all counted for the purpose of holding a seat in the national assembly, it can perpetrate a fraud on every legally constituted congressional district in the United States, and there is no security for representative government in any corner of the land. If any class or race can be permanently set apart from and pushed down below the rest in political and civil rights, so may any other class or race when it shall incur the displeasure of its more powerful associates, and we may say farewell at once to the principles on which we have counted for our safety.

We are confronted not by a theory but by a fact. That fact is the deliberate and avowed exclusion of a whole race of our fellow citizens from their constitutional rights, accompanied by the announcement that that exclusion must and shall be permanent. It is not that the Negro is ignorant, nor that he is poor, nor that he is vicious, but that he is a Negro. Even when he is good and learned and rich, he must still be excluded because he is still a Negro. That is the proposition, and that it is which makes it the duty of all who dissent from such a doctrine to make their dissent known and to make it uncompromising and clear.

If the southern states were only taking the ground that all voters white and black alike must possess certain high qualifications in property and education, the situation would not be what it is. Such restrictions might result in the exclusion of the great mass of colored men as it would result in the exclusion of large numbers of the white. Yet we might well wait for the effects of time. If any indication were to be found that the South is looking forward to a day when the colored man shall exercise his political rights and that it is providing some process, no matter how slow and gradual. by which that result may be attained, it might be our patriotic duty to hold our peace. But when no such indication is to be found, when no encouragement is held out that the Negro shall ever have any, even the slightest, part in the government under which he lives, patriotic duty forbids that we should be silent. When will there be any change—why should there be any change—as long as the whole country, North as well as South, acquiesces in the present order?

But there is a still deeper consequence involved. If laws can be made and enforced which every child knows were intended to deprive and do in fact deprive millions of American citizens of the rights guaranteed them by the Constitution of their country, it is vain to call on men to reverence the law, and when we swear to the Constitution we swear to a rotten reed. "When the Son of Man cometh shall He find faith on the earth?" That was the old prophetic question. Not faith in the mystic spiritual sense but *fides,* good faith, common honesty. When multitudes of men take an oath which on their own confession they have no thought of keeping, the public conscience is debased and the bond that holds society together is well nigh dissolved. The grossest barbarian that ever shed human blood to solemnize his oath has had some form of words that would bind his darkened conscience, and to break which he counted as damnation. It was left for the nineteenth Christian century to exhibit the spectacle of thousands of civilized men taking upon their lips an oath, in the most solemn form of their religion, which they themselves publicly and shamelessly admit they never intended to observe. From such a position it is but a short step to verdicts on the unwritten law and trial and execution by the mob. When the Constitution is defied it can make no essential difference whether that defiance is expressed in Tillman's coarse and brutal words, "To hell with the Constitution," or is couched in some honeyed, euphemistic phrase that appeals to Anglo-Saxon prejudice and pride. In either case the thing is done.

It is a fitting day for such a subject. It has become the fashion of recent years to treat the Civil War as nothing but a political contest, ignoring the tremendous moral issues that alone justified its sacrifices. But read Lincoln's second inaugural, where he spoke as the prophet of his people and uttered the deep secret of the conflict. It will not do to shut our eyes to the real causes and results of the war—especially now when northern indifference and southern injustice strike hands to keep the black race in a new bondage as helpless and hopeless as the old. As a member of the white race and turning for the moment to white men, I say that our race will deserve any calamity the presence of the black race may bring.

We brought it here by theft and force. We owed it liberty and we gave it a chain. We owe it light and we give it darkness. We owe it opportunity and we hedge it round with· restraints. We owe it the court-house and we give it the lynching tree. We owe it an example of order and self control; we give it an example of lawlessness and hate. We are sowing the wind and if we reap the whirlwind we shall have ourselves to blame.

The strong imagine they have a mortgage upon the weak, but in the world of morals it is the other way. We complain that virtue and intelligence cannot be safe in the neighborhood of ignorance and vice. God means that it should be so. So does he take bonds from the mighty to do justice by the weak. Shame on the race that holds in its hands the wealth of the continent and carries in its brain the accumulated culture of the centuries and yet, refusing to lift ignorance and vice to the level of enlightenment and virtue, makes that ignorance and vice an excuse for the denial of human rights. Never until the white man has spent his last surplus dollar and ex-hausted the last faculty of his brain in the effort to lift up his weaker brother—never until then can he stand in the presence of infinite justice and complain of the ignorance or the criminality of the black.

It is really a contest between caste and equality—a contest as old as the world and possibly as permanent. The spirit of caste is nothing else than that self worship that is fostered and gratified when it can look down upon another. The secret of caste is inordinate self love and pride. It can find no welcome in the heart where the Son of Man is made at home. Underneath every political or social phase of the **subj**ect lies the profounder phase which makes it a question of duty and of true religion. If we can do nothing else, we can at least, on this day of sacred memories, purify our ideals, and test our conduct by them. We do not make our ideals, our ideals make us. America did not choose the great doctrine of equal rights—that immortal truth chose America. It has moulded her from the beginning; it will mould her until the end; or if it cannot it will cast her off with the wreckage of the past and take up some other nation that shall be found worthy.

There is a power that has been working here from the beginning. It is the power that will be working here when you and I are gone. It is the power whose purpose is that all men shall be free. Various races have at various times flattered themselves that they were a chosen people. But if history shows anything it shows that a nation is nothing but a tool in the hand of the Almighty. If it serves His purpose it is used. If it breaks in His hand it is thrown away, and another is chosen in its stead. If this nation has any mission it is to make the Declaration of Independence good—that and the three great amendments to the Constitution which were the logical result of that sublime pledge. It is true those amendments were adopted in a glow of idealism. But so was the Declaration itself. It is true they have not been lived up to any more than the Declaration was lived up to in the first seventy years of the republic. But now as then and at all other times the test of our institutions, both of their power to last and of their worthiness to last, is simply and solely this: Do they serve to keep the rights of men sacred and secure?

Address of

John T. Milholland

of the

Constitution League, New York

Frankly it must be said the forces at work for the colored man's uplift in the South are not the prevailing forces. The sentiment for his just, equitable treatment, for the vindication of his constitutional rights as a citizen and a man is neither yet strong enough nor sufficiently widespread to be compared for an instant with the Satanic energies behind that avowed determination to crush him down again to the low level of physical as well as political slavery. To deny this is to blind one's self to the every day evidence that has been multiplying with cumulative effect since the surrender of Lee at Appomattox.

Mr. Chairman, the value of the Georgia Railroad strike as an illuminant of the situation cannot easily be exaggerated. It puts the whole case in diamond light, revealing with the clearness of noonday the manifest tendency towards the utter degradation of the Negro about which we of the Constitution League and other disturbed spirits have been preaching and prophesying these many years.

Deplorable as it is, I welcome it. Disgraceful to the South that permits it; disgraceful to these northern trades unions that have aided and directed this latest conspiracy against the rights of man; a blot on the escutcheon of our Republic and a shame to modern civilization; nevertheless, I for one, am glad that it has come to pass. Such results were and are inevitable. Bad as they are, worse will follow unless this great nation opens its eyes to the actualities that confront it upon this Memorial day, this day that brings back to us those momentous times that tried men's souls but warmed all hearts, those rays of great misery but of a great hope that have been succeeded so soon by the days of forgetfulness!

Conditions, I repeat, desperate as they are in the South must grow worse before they grow better. I said this years ago when the Republican traitors, leaders at Washington, aided by misguided zealots elsewhere, refused to see anything very serious in the failure of the bill for honest Federal elections in the South or the defeat of the Blair education measure—a calamity that has cost the South twenty years of genuine progress; in the nullification by southern states of the great war amendments to the Constitution, those sublime declarations which represent the highwater mark of American statesmanship, the loftiest declaration of human rights that has ever been promulgated by any national lawmaking assembly since the years of jubilee rang out among the hills of old Judea "proclaiming liberty throughout the land and to the inhabitants thereof."

The Negro's condition, I contend, in this country is growing worse every year. He is standing on the very threshold of a physical slavery almost as bad and hopeless as that from which he was emancipated by one of the bloodiest wars ever waged in Christendom. Practically a political serf in a dozen states, without right to vote or liberty to speak; trial by a jury of his peers denied him, and in such imminent danger of lynching that he lives under a reign of terror as awful as that inspired by Ku-Klux depredations or the old Spanish Inquisition—to talk about such a man enjoying the liberty that is supposed to be the normal condition of every American citizen is to fly in the face of truth and proclaim ·oneself incapable of observation.

Passing the bloody massacres of the Reconstruction period, we have seen year after year, for nearly two decades, no less than three citizens every week lynched or burned or shot to death without the semblance of judicial procedure to ascertain their guilt or innocence. And yet these mob murders do not reveal the worst of it; they only suggest the brutal tyranny, the horrible beatings of defenseless men and boys, girls and women; the humiliations of mind and hearts, sensitive by nature and cultivation; the breaking of strong men's wills and the unspeakable degradations of mothers and daughters whose sons and husbands are powerless to afford them the protection that is even denied them by the law.

Senator Tillman of South Carolina is not an authority I quote but what he says on this point is so thoroughly in accordance with known facts as to make this testimony relevant and of value. On July 20, 1907, he declared in the United States Senate: "Race hatred grows day by day. There is no man who is honest, going through the South and conversing with the white people and blacks, but will return and tell you this is true. Then I say to you of the North who are the rulers of the land, who can change this or do something to relieve conditions, what are you going to do about it? Are you going to sit .quiet? If nothing else will cause you to think, I notify you, what you already know, that there are a billion dollars or more of northern capital invested in the South in railroads, in mines, in forests, in farm lands, and self interest, which fact if nothing else, ought to make you set about hunting some remedy for this terrible situation. Therefore we say to you it is your duty to do something. It is your duty to move. It is your duty to begin the discussion. For the time being the South is occupying an attitude of constant friction, race riot, butchery, murder of whites by blacks and blacks by whites, the inevitable, irresponsible conflict."

This is a note different from that usually sounded at Carnegie Hall and Tremont Temple, but every man familiar with the case knows that the South Carolina Senator, in this instance at least, speaks the truth, and because it is the truth, I think the *raison d'être* of this conference has been sufficiently established.

THE RACE PROBLEM

Jenkins Lloyd Jones

of

Chicago

The civilized world, with impressive unanimity and inspiring heartiness, has just been celebrating the centennial of the birth of him who signed the Emancipation Proclamation. When the second centennial comes round this document will be more prized and better known than now. Many things conspire in these days to obscure the light that should and will emanate through all time from this glow point in the history of the United States.

The character and place of Abraham Lincoln in history can never be understood if the title of Emancipator is ignored, evaded or minimized. "Emancipator" is the key-word to the great President, and the Emancipation Proclamation is the pivotal point not only in the war but in the history of the United States. We ought all to see it now, but it took a poet's vision to see it then.

Let apologists and politicians North or South trace the inspirations of the civil war to petty and secondary causes, the only adequate explanation of the acceptance of war by the unwarlike people of the North is found in the word "Liberty," and so far as ethical questions can be settled by war—alas, how little can be done that way—the human theory of the Negro was vindicated. It was an awful price to pay, but for myself I deem the abolition of the human auction block cheap at any price; much as I hate war, I would accept the bitter experience again if the end could not be attained otherwise. I would march every foot of the weary ground that I traversed from 1862 to 1865 for the sake of knowing that a slave-mother's child could become the guest of English nobility, the poet laureate of the Negro race, deserving and receiving the praise that belongs to a poet, irrespective of rank or color. With prophetic insight did the Great Emancipator say of the war: "Yet, if God wills that it continue until all the wealth 'piled by the bondman's two hundred and fifty years of unrequited toil shall be sunk, and until every drop of blood drawn with the lash shall be paid by another drawn with the sword, as was said three thousand years ago, so still it must be said, 'The judgments of the Lord are true and righteous altogether.'"

But alas, by what slow processes do liberty and justice come to their own? There has come a recrudescence of the ethnology of slavery under the guise of a superficial science. In many quarters a painful reaction has come that has silenced the voice of religion, confused the problems at the ballot, and intimidated the one-time champions of the despised race. We still hear preachers in the pulpit pleading for segregation; educators deploring the education of the black; legislators, by downright subterfuge and the tricks of circumlocution which only a demagogue can use, disfranchising those who were enfranchised by the decrees of war, the acts of Congress, and the signature of the great emancipator.

All this in the face of the cold, hard facts that prove the colored man worthy the confidence placed in him by those who died for his freedom. He has justified the momentous signature, the holiest autograph in American history—that attached to the Emancipation Proclamation. In the space of a short half-century, and that demoralized by war, the colored man is on his way towards the full justification of the Thirteenth, Fourteenth and Fifteenth Amendments of the Constitution. The story of his emancipation is outdone by the still more wonderful story of his education. Civilization offers no parallel to the rise of the enslaved race. The memory of Lincoln has been glorified and most splendidly vindicated by the triumph of the black man.

Lincoln's work cannot be undone. There is no ground for despondency, but there is for vigilance. Timidity, racial prejudice, pride, social cowardice and inherited bias still combine to create lines where none exist, perpetrate prejudices unjustified, and foster assumptions unwarranted by science and condemned by religion.

The ante-bellum cry was "Do not interfere with our peculiar institutions." There is a post-bellum prattle about southern problems being handled by southern people. This assembly should send forth the note, far and clear, that there is no North or South in freedom now, any more than was there in '65. In times of peace, as in times of war, the question of justice knows no state limits. In the eyes of enlightened statesmanship and in the eyes of God, the status of the Negro in New Orleans is the same as that of the Negro in Chicago. He demands a square deal, and only a square deal, in the one place as in the other. The Negro is a candidate now as always, North, South, here, everywhere, for all that nature and human nature can fit him for, and all the legal sophistries, and legislative double-dealings that breed injustice towards him are a greater menace to the white perpetrators thereof than to the black victims of the same.

There are no "southern problems" that are not national; no "race problems" that are not lost in human problems. Providence is kinder to the oppressed than to the oppressor; the wronged than the wronger. The rise of the black man under the inspiration of freedom is surely inevitable, inspiring. The emancipation of the white man, his former master and his descendants, is perhaps a slower process; one that awakens deeper anxiety, and the failure of which is a far greater menace to the growth and prosperity of our nation.

To talk of a "southern problem" to-day, as distinguished from the "northern problem"; for any section of this country to ask to be let alone to adjust its own social affairs, is harking back to an old régime, forever past. So far as there is a Negro problem, whether it springs from the incapacity or depravity of black men or the narrowness, arrogance and commercial conceit of the white man, like Eliza in the story, it has crossed the Ohio River on floating ice. Mob violence, brutal lynchings and lawless panics appear in Illinois as in South Carolina; they have disgraced the records of courts and stained the soil with blood, in Ohio as in Mississippi. The supremacy of the national government and the urgency of national education and national legislation, in social as well as commercial adjustments, are becoming daily more imperious.

A limited suffrage may be good statesmanship; we only demand that that limitation be honestly stated and impartially enforced. It may be wise under some conditions to separate white and black children in the schools, but for the legislature of Kentucky to call upon the trustees of Berea to violate their sacred trust to the dead, to disturb the benign traditions and precedents of decades, and to shut the doors of the college against diligent, law-abiding and self-respecting students because of a tint in the skin and a kink in the hair, though the tint and the kink be ameliorated by ninety per cent. of blood drawn from the veins of the Kentucky chivalry that breeds nothing meaner than "colonels," is an indignity to justice, a violation of the fundamental principles of democracy and the more precious decrees written in the blood of the heroes of '76 and of '61 to '65.

We should demand that the race theories born of ignorance and prejudice be revised by the latest science; that no illegitimacy of parentage be allowed to interfere with the divine legitimacy of children; that womanhood be protected by statute and public sentiment, whatever its complexion; that virginity be held as sacred in the colored as the white maiden and the violators thereof be held with equal severity by law and by public sentiment, whether they be white or black. We should call for impartial enforcement of statute rights of all citizens of any color. We protest against decreed distinctions and gradations of rights under the Constitution of the United States and declare there are no privileges according to the laws and constitution of the United States vouchsafed to the black man in Minnesota that are not decreed in Louisiana. These demands are imperative. The situation is urgent.

Out of our dire disgraces the urgent needs, the pathetic cries of the victims of past tyranny and present prejudices, and the more pathetic fears, social anxieties and political confusions of the white victims of past wrongs, there must rise a new movement that will seize the fallen flag and hold it aloft once more, bearing it forward until the nation is awakened and liberty and justice find fresh endorsement, and until community life shall overreach sect, party, industrial, or racial lines. In this movement state lines must fade in the presence of national inspirations and obligations, and national boundaries will sink out of sight in the presence of international sympathy and confidence.

It is to help on such a movement, is it not, that we are here?

IS THE SOUTHERN POSITION
ANGLO-SAXON?

John Spencer Bassett

Professor of History

Smith College

There is such a thing as the Anglo-Saxon attitude toward inferiors. By observing the feelings on the subject in the places in which the English stock has ruled
inferiors we may have the general features of this Anglo-
Saxon attitude. And when this has been found it will
be seen that the southerner goes somewhat further in
repression than the Englishman, and that this surplusage
is the part of the southern race antipathy which appears
most artificial. It is an outgrowth of peculiar historical
conditions, and we may hope to lessen its intensity.

Cape Colony is that British possession in which conditions with reference to the Negro are most like those
in our southern states. In each locality the Negro strikes
the white man in much the same way. It is the recoil
of the superior from the inferior. But in Africa the
aversion is not solidified as in the South. In one place
the individual white man determines his attitude toward
the black man, in the other the community determines it,
and woe to him who disputes the decision. In one place,
in spite of a large number who are antagonistic to Negro
development there are many who seek to bring it about,
and they are allowed to do what they choose. In the
other there is a public opinion about the Negro, and its
dictum is final. In one a Negro of great capacity may

rise out of the sphere of inferiority without a great shock to the whites around him; in the other he may rise till he is esteemed great in all the rest of the world, but he will ever have "the place" of the most inferior member of his race in the eyes of his white neighbors.

Mr. Bryce gives us some good illustrations of the feeling in Cape Colony. For example, a gentleman there may invite an educated Negro to dinner, but before doing so he will ask his white guests if they object to such company. Nor does it happen that he loses position in society because he has been host to a native. He is eligible thereafter as a guest himself at the home of those who would not accept his invitation under the conditions specified. The same is true as to intermarriage: it occurs rarely and there is no law against it. Sometimes a poor white man will work for a Negro who has employment for him. Generally the children of the two races attend separate schools; but it happens at times that poor white people send their children to schools for blacks because the fees are smaller and no one objects. White people are concerned in philanthropic work for blacks, acting individually and as churches, and by so doing they do *not* lose their efficiency in other work for and with white people. Social relations with Negroes are not desired by the majority of the whites but those who oppose such relations do not think the safety of society demands that the advocates of other views be held as enemies of the public good. On this subject people seem to think that the best safety of the public lies in allowing a man to believe as he chooses without making him pay any penalty.

Now, I do not say that this is a desirable thing. It may or may not be so; but my present contention is that this is entirely unlike the position of our South. And since the conditions are relatively the same in Jamaica and in other British colonies in which whites rule blacks,

I think it fair to say that it stands for the Anglo-Saxon attitude toward the Negro. That is to say, the British are unwilling to accept the inferior as an equal, but they are willing to try to make him equal, and their sense of fair play tolerates and even applauds the successful efforts to raise him above himself. It is a doctrine which sprang from the English instinct of liberty, and it was brought to America by the British founders.

Thus it happened that the Methodist and Missionary Baptist churches became the strongest popular religious organizations in the South, and they so remained throughout the eighteenth century. Although others labored as they could these two popular churches were particularly active in work for the Negro. In true Anglo-Saxon spirit they took him into the churches and in exceptional cases they allowed him to preach, but they did not give him the right to hold office. They believed, and he acquiesced in it, that he was not capable of directing the affairs of the church. This mingling of blacks and whites in a field of common concern was the best guarantee of mutual peace and sympathy; and since religion was the sphere of mental activity at which the white man's ideals were most likely to enter the Negro's life, this association in the churches promised much for the future. When the nineteenth century began, and for three decades thereafter, the whites had the Anglo-Saxon attitude toward the Negro. They sought to develop him, they recognized his inferiority in the mass while they encouraged all efforts in the individual which seemed to work for his uplift. Some illustrations of this state of affairs will show how harmonious the situation was at this time.

The position of the southern churches at this time has its parallel in that of some of the leading public men. Washington and many prominent Virginians were well known for their mild views of the Negro. In 1791, Jef-

ferson, secretary of state, appointed a Negro mathematician to office in his department because he wanted to see
if a Negro would succeed in that capacity. His letter
to a gentleman in France telling of the matter shows
that he did not disapprove of Negro office-holders. And
it was under Andrew Jackson, the second founder of the
Democratic party, that Negroes, so far as I can learn,
were first received at a social function in the White
House.

Now these incidents do not prove everything, but they
show that public opinion in 1791 and in 1829 was not
like public opinion in the South at present. All that I
claim is that in the first three decades of the nineteenth
century the Southern whites had the typical English attitude toward the Negro. They recognized his inferiority, they sought to secure his development, and that pain-
fully solid opinion which demands that white hands shall
never touch black ones had not come into existence. If
the problem of the inferior could have been worked out
under this gentler system, this conference, probably,
would not have been called. But mild measures could
not be followed. To destroy slavery was of greater immediate importance than to develop the Negro. About
1830 the storm began which was to secure emancipation
and the blue sky has been darkened ever since. It was
perhaps a necessary storm, but it has been unnecessarily
prolonged.

The controversy which was to work so much that was
good and so much that was not good for the Negro was
at first concerned with slavery; since 1865 it has been concerned with the position of the Negro. The slavery
problem and the Negro problem are distinct by nature,
but in their development in America one ran into the
other. Northern men declared that slavery wronged the
Negro by taking from him his inalienable rights; southern men replied that the Negro had no inalienable rights

and that slavery was the condition best suited for his development. And it happened that by a process of action and reaction each side became more emphatic in its assertions until at last one was declaring for Negro suffrage, thus ennobling the inferior to the position of equal citizenship, and the other was declaring that slavery was a divinely appointed institution. Southern churches which in 1800 worked for the conversion of Negroes and taught that slavery was an evil were in 1850 teaching that the African was divinely ordained to bondage; and the most radical of Southerners were beginning to ask if he had any soul which God was bound to respect. It was a conviction which did not rest on failure in the efforts to elevate him but which grew out of a heated condition of the public mind in the great sectional controversy.

Then came the war with its failures and reconstruction with its fury. Whether we condemn or approve Negro suffrage which the North forced on the South while it could, we shall see that it did not improve the South's opinion of the Negro. From 1830 to 1909 is a long period. There is not a man living in the South to-day who remembers the time when the Negro question was not associated with passion. The people there not only have forgotten that they ever planned and strove to develop the race in the old English way, but they have difficulty to believe the historian when he proves it from their own history. They have not thought it possible to return to the former attitude, and yet what has been done can be done again.

If we could return to the attitude which existed in the days of saner conditions, the days of Jefferson and Washington, we should not have social intermingling of the races. The difference between that condition and the present would be in the absence of friction. A white man would not hate a Negro because he was a Negro, and a black man would not hate a white man because he was white. We should then lose that apprehension, as old as slavery, that some day there will come a great bloody struggle between the two hostile races, a struggle whose great probability lies in the habitual anticipation of it.

The North and the South are jointly responsible for the struggle which brought race antipathy to its present condition; and they have joint responsibility for its removal. The best thing they can do is to let the fires go out. But patience is not our only obligation. There ought also to be wise and persistent effort for Negro uplift. And this is a duty which ought to fall on the South as well as on the North. People who are striving to help the Negro will not hate him. If this conference can suggest some means of bringing the many efforts of the North to improve the condition of the Negro into touch with the southern whites, it will do the best day's work done in many a month in the cause of the black man's progress. For example, if the missionary agencies in a southern state should hold a conference to consider their own work in which they could induce southern clergymen to take part, there would be laid the foundation of mutual understanding and good will, and it would result beneficially to all concerned. If such harmony can be obtained, we shall be in a fair way to return to the old Anglo-Saxon attitude, which sprang from English love of fair play, and which is only obscured by events which in their nature are transitory.

EVOLUTION OF THE RACE PROBLEM

W. E. B. DuBois

Professor of Economics

Atlanta University

Those who complain that the Negro problem is always with us and apparently insoluble must not forget that under this vague and general designation are gathered many social problems and many phases of the same problem; that these problems and phases have passed through a great evolutionary circle and that to-day especially one may clearly see a repetition, vaster but similar, of the great cycle of the past.

That problem of the past, so far as the black American was concerned, began with caste—a definite place preordained in custom, law and religion where all men of black blood must be thrust. To be sure, this caste idea as applied to blacks was no sudden, full grown conception, for the enslavement of the workers was an idea which America inherited from Europe and was not synonymous for many years with the enslavement of the blacks, although the blacks were the chief workers. Men came to the idea of exclusive black slavery by gradually enslaving the workers, as was the world's long custom, and then gradually conceiving certain sorts of work and certain colors of men as necessarily connected. It was, when once set up definitely in the southern slave system, a logically cohering whole which the simplest social philosopher could easily grasp and state. The difficulty was it was too simple to be either just or true. Human nature is not simple and any classification that roughly divides men into good and bad, superior and inferior, slave and free, is and must ever be ludicrously untrue and universally dangerous as a permanent exhaustive classification. So in the southern slave system the thing that from the first damned it was the free Negro—the Negro legally free, the Negro economically free and the Negro spiritually free.

How was the Negro to be treated and conceived of who was legally free? At first with perfect naturalness he was treated as a man—he voted in Massachusetts and in South Carolina, in New York and Virginia; he intermarried with black and white, he claimed and received his civil rights—all this until the caste of color was so turned as to correspond with the caste of work and enslave not only slaves but black men who were not slaves. Even this system, however, was unable to ensure complete economic dependence on the part of all black men; there were continually artisans, foremen and skilled servants who became economically too valuable to be slaves. In vain were laws hurled at Negro intelligence and responsibility; black men continued to hire their time and to steal some smattering of knowledge, and it was this fact that became the gravest menace to the slave system. But even legal and economic freedom was not so dangerous to slavery as the free spirit which continually cropped out among men fated to be slaves: they thought, they dreamed, they aspired, they resisted. In vain were they beaten, sold south and killed, the ranks were continually filled with others and they either led revolt at home or ran away to the North, and these by showing their human qualities continually gave the lie to the slave assumption. Thus it was the free Negro in these manifold phases of his appearance who hastened the economic crisis which killed slavery and who made it impossible to make the caste of work and the caste of color correspond, and who became at once the promise and excuse of those who forced the critical revolution.

To-day in larger cycle and more intricate detail we are passing through certain phases of a similar evolution. To-day we have the caste idea—again not a sudden full grown conception but one being insidiously but consciously and persistently pressed upon the nation. The steps toward it which are being taken are: first, political disfranchisement, then vocational education with the distinct idea of narrowing to the uttermost the vocations in view, and finally a curtailment of civil freedom of travel, association, and entertainment, in systematic effort to instill contempt and kill self-respect.

Here then is the new slavery of black men in America —a new attempt to make degradation of social condition correspond with certain physical characteristics—not to be sure fully realized as yet, and probably unable for reasons of social development ever to become as systematized as the economic and physical slavery of the past— and yet realized to an extent almost unbelievable by those who have not taken the pains to study the facts—to an extent which makes the lives of thinking black men in this land a perpetual martyrdom.

But right here as in the past stands in the path of this idea the figure of this same thinking black man—this new freedman. This freedman again as in the past presents himself as free in varying phases: there is the free black voter of the North and border states whose power is far more tremendous than even he dare think so that he is afraid to use it; there is the black man who has accomplished economic freedom and who by working himself into the vast industrial development of the nation is to-day accumulating property at a rate that is simply astounding. And finally tnere is the small but growing number of black men emerging into spiritual freedom and becoming participators and freemen of the kingdom of culture around which it is so singularly difficult to set metes and bounds, and who in art, science and literature are making their modest but ineffaceable mark.

The question is what is the significance of this group of men for the future of the caste programme and for the future social development of America? In order to answer this question intelligently let us retrace our steps and follow more carefully the details of the proposed programme of renewed caste in America. This programme when one comes to define and state it is elusive. There are even those who deny its existence as a definite consciously conceived plan of action. But, certain it is, there is growing unanimity of a peculiar sort on certain matters. And this unanimity is centering about three propositions:

1. That it was a mistake to give Negroes the ballot.
2. That Negroes are essentially an inferior race.
3. That the only permanent settlement of the race problem will be open and legal recognition of this inferiority.

When now a modern nation condemns ten million of its fellows to such a fate it would be supposed that this conclusion has been reluctantly forced upon them after a careful study and weighing of the facts. This, however, is not the case in the Negro problem. On the contrary there has been manifest a singular reluctance and indisposition carefully to study the Negro problem. Ask the average American: Why should the ballot have been withheld from the Negro, and he will answer: "Because he wasn't fit for it." But that is not a sufficient answer: first, because few newly enfranchised groups of the most successful democracies have been fit for the ballot when it was first given, and secondly, because there were Negroes in the United States fit for the ballot in 1870. Moreover the political philosophy that condemns out of hand the Fifteenth Amendment does not often stop to think that the problem before the American nation 1865-1870 was not a simple problem of fixing the qualifications of voters. It was, on the contrary, the immensely more complicated problem of enforcing a vast social and economic revolution on a people determined not to submit to it. Whenever a moral reform is forced on a people from without there ensue complicated and tremendous problems, whether that reform is the correction of the abuse of alcohol, the abolition of child labor or the emancipation of slaves. The enforcement of such a reform will strain every nerve of the nation and the real question is not: Is it a good thing to strain the framework of the nation but rather: Is slavery so dangerous a thing that sudden enfranchisement of the ex-slaves is too great a price to pay for its abolition?

To be sure there are those who profess to think that the white South of its own initiative after the war, with the whole of the wealth, intelligence and law-making power in its hands, would have freely emancipated its slaves in obedience to a decree from Washington, just as there are those who would entrust the regulation of the whiskey traffic to saloon keepers and the bettering of the conditions of child labor to the employers. It is no attack on the South or on saloon keepers or on employers to say that such a reform from such a source is unthinkable. It is simply human nature that men trained to a social system or condition should be the last to be entirely entrusted with its reformation. It was, then, not the Emancipation Proclamation but the Fifteenth Amendment that made slavery impossible in the United States and those that object to the Fifteenth Amendment have simply this question to answer: Which was best, slavery or ignorant Negro voters? The answer is clear as day: Negro voters never did anything as bad as slavery. If they were guilty of all the crimes charged to them by the wildest enemies, even then what they did was less dangerous, less evil and less cruel than the system of slavery whose death knell they struck.   And when in addition to this we remember that the black voters of the South established the public schools, gave the poor whites the ballot, modernized the penal code and put on the statute books of the South page after page of legislation that still stands to-day—when we remember this, we have a right to conclude that the Fifteenth Amendment was a wise and far-sighted piece of statesmanship.

But to-day the men who oppose the right of Negroes to vote are no longer doing so on the ground of ignorance, and with good reason, for to-day a majority and an appreciable majority of the black men of the South twenty-one years of age and over can read and write.   In other words, the bottom has been clean knocked out of their ignorance argument and yet the fact has elicited scarcely a loud remark.

Indeed we black men are continually puzzled by the easy almost unconscious way in which our detractors change their ground.   Before emancipation it was stated and reiterated with bitter emphasis and absolute confidence that a free Negro would prove to be a shiftless scamp, a barbarian and a cannibal reverting to savagery and doomed to death.   We forget to-day that from 1830 to 1860 there was not a statement made by the masters of slaves more often reiterated than this, and more dogmatically and absolutely stated.   After emancipation, for twenty years and more, so many people looked for the fulfilment of the prophecy that many actually saw it and we heard and kept hearing and now and then still hear that the Negro to-day is worse off than in slavery days.   Then, as this statement grew less and less plausible, its place came to be taken by other assumptions. When a Louisiana senator saw the first Negro school he stopped and said: "This is the climax of foolishness!" The Negro could not be educated—he could imitate like a parrot but real mental development was impossible.

Then, when Negroes did learn some things, it was said that education spoiled them; they can learn but it does them no practical good; the young educated Negroes become criminals—they neither save nor work, they are shiftless and lazy. Now to-day are coming uncomfortable facts for this theory. The generation now working and saving is post-bellum and yet no sooner does it come on the stage than accumulated property goes on at an accelerated pace so far as we have measurements. In Georgia the increase of property among Negroes in the last ten years has been 83%. But no sooner do facts like these come to the fore than again the ground of opposition subtly shifts and this last shifting has been so gradual and so insidious that the Negro and his friends are still answering arguments that are no longer being pushed. The most subtle enemies of democracy and the most persistent advocates of the color line admit almost contemptuously most that their forebears strenuously denied: the Negroes have progressed since slavery, they are accumulating some property, some of them work readily and they are susceptible of elementary training; but, they say, all thought of treating black men like white men must be abandoned. They are an inferior stock of men, limited in attainment by nature. You cannot legislate against nature, and philanthropy is powerless against deficient cerebral development.

To realize the full weight of this argument recall to mind a character like John Brown and contrast his attitude with the attitude of to-day. John Brown loved his neighbor as himself. He could not endure, therefore, to see his neighbor poor, unfortunate or oppressed. This natural sympathy was strengthened by a saturation in Hebrew religion which stressed the personal responsibility of every man's soul to a just God. To this religion of equality and sympathy with misfortune, was added the strong influence of the social doctrines of the French Revolution with its emphasis on freedom and power in political life. And on all this was built John Brown's own inchoate but growing belief in a juster and more equal distribution of property. From all this John Brown concluded—and acted on that conclusion—that all men were created free and equal and that the cost of liberty was less than the price of repression. Up to the time of John Brown's death this doctrine was a growing, conquering social thing. Since then there has come a change and many would rightly find reason for that change in the coincidence that the year John Brown suffered martyrdom was the year that first published the Origin of Species. Since that day tremendous scientific and economic advance has been accompanied by distinct signs of moral change in social philosophy; strong arguments have been made for the fostering of war, the social utility of human degradation and disease, and the inevitable and known inferiority of certain classes and races of men. While such arguments have not stopped the efforts of the advocates of peace, the workers for social uplift and the believers in human brotherhood, they have, it must be confessed, often made their voices falter and tinged their arguments with apology.

Why is this? It is because the splendid scientific work of Darwin, Weissman, Galton and others has been widely and popularly interpreted as meaning that there is such essential and inevitable inequality among men and races of men as no philanthropy can or ought to eliminate; that civilization is a struggle for existence whereby the weaker nations and individuals will gradually succumb and the strong will inherit the earth. With this interpretation has gone the silent assumption that the white European stock represents the strong surviving peoples and that the swarthy, yellow and black peoples are the ones rightly doomed to eventual extinction.

One can easily see what influence such a doctrine would have on the race problem in America. It meant moral revolution in the attitude of the nation. Those that stepped into the pathway marked by the early abolitionists faltered and large numbers turned back. They said: They were good men—even great, but they have no message for us to-day—John Brown was a "belated covenanter," William Lloyd Garrison was an anachronism in the age of Darwin—men who gave their lives to lift not the unlifted but the unliftable. We have, consequently, the present reaction—a reaction which says in effect: Keep these black people in their places, and do not attempt to treat a Negro simply as a white man with a black face; to do this would mean moral deterioration of the race and nation—a fate against which a divine racial prejudice is successfully fighting. This is the attitude of the larger portion of the thinking nation to-day.

It is not, however, an attitude that has brought mental rest or social peace. On the contrary, it is to-day involving a degree of moral strain and political and social anomaly that gives the wisest pause. The chief difficulty has been that the natural place in which, by scientific law, the black race in America should stay cannot easily be determined. To be sure, the freedmen did not, as the philanthropists of the sixties apparently expected, step in forty years from slavery to nineteenth century civilization. Neither, on the other hand, did they, as the ex-masters confidently predicted, retrograde and die. Contrary to both these views, they chose a third and apparently quite unawaited way: from the great, sluggish, almost imperceptibly moving mass they sent off larger and larger numbers of faithful workmen and artisans, some merchants and professional men, and even men of educational ability and discernment. They developed in a generation no world geniuses, no millionaires, no captains of industry, no artists of first rank; but they did in forty years get rid of the larger part of their illiteracy, accumulate a half billion of property in small homesteads and gained now and then respectful attention in the world's ears and eyes. It has been argued that this progress of the black man in America is due to the exceptional men among them and does not measure the ability of the mass. Such admission is, however, fatal to the whole argument. If the doomed races of men are going to develop exceptions to the rule of inferiority then no law, scientific or moral, should or can proscribe the race as such.

To meet this difficulty in racial philosophy a step has been taken in America fraught with the gravest social consequences to the world and threatening not simply the political but the moral integrity of the nation: that step is to deny in the case of black men the validity of those evidences of culture, ability and decency which are accepted unquestioningly in the case of other people, and by vague assertion, unprovable assumption, unjust emphasis, and now and then by deliberate untruth, to secure not only the continued proscription of these people, but by caste distinction to shut in the faces of their rising classes many of the paths to further advance.

When a social policy based on a supposed scientific sanction leads to such a moral anomaly it is time to examine rather carefully the logical foundations of the argument. And so soon as we do this many things are clear. First, assuming that there are certain stocks of human beings whose elimination the best welfare of the world demands; it is certainly questionable if these stocks include the majority of mankind and it is indefensible and monstrous to pretend that we know to-day with any reasonable certainty which these stocks are. We can point to degenerate individuals and families here and there among all races, but there is not the slightest warrant for assuming that there do not exist among the Chinese and Hindus, the African Bantus and American Indians as lofty possibilities of human culture as any European race has ever exhibited. It is, to be sure, puzzling to know why the Soudan should linger a thousand years in culture behind the valley of the Seine, but it is no more puzzling than the fact that the valley of the Thames was miserably backward as compared with the banks of the Tiber. Climate, human contact, facilities of communication, and what we call accident have played great part in the rise of culture among nations: to ignore these and to assert dogmatically that the present distribution of culture is a fair index of the distribution of human ability and desert is to make an assertion for which there is not the slightest scientific warrant.

What the age of Darwin has done is to add to the eighteenth century idea of individual worth the complementary idea of physical immortality of the human race. And this, far from annulling or contracting the idea of human freedom, rather emphasizes its necessity and eternal possibility—the boundlessness and endlessness of possible human achievement. Freedom has come to mean not individual caprice or aberration but social self-realization in an endless chain of selves, and freedom for such development is not the denial but the central assertion of the evolutionary theory. So, too, the doctrine of human equality passes through the fire of scientific inquiry not obliterated but transfigured; not equality of present attainment but equality of opportunity for unbounded future attainment is the rightful demand of mankind.

What now does the present hegemony of the white races threaten? It threatens by the means of brute force a survival of some of the worst stocks of mankind. It attempts to people the best part of the earth and put in absolute authority over the rest not only, and indeed not mainly, the culture of Europe, but its greed and degradation—not only some representatives of the best stocks of the west end of London, upper New York and the Champs Elysées but also, and in as large, if not larger, numbers, the worst stocks of Whitechapel, the East Side and Montmartre; and it attempts to make the slums of white society in all cases and under all circumstances the superior of any colored group, no matter what its ability or culture; it attempts to put the intelligent, property holding, efficient Negroes of the South under the heels and at the absolute mercy of such constituencies as Tillman, Vardaman and Jeff Davis represent.

To be sure, this outrageous programme of wholesale human degeneration is not outspoken yet save in the backward civilizations of the southern United States, South Africa and Australia. But its enunciation is listened to with respect and tolerance in England, Germany and the northern states and nowhere with more equanimity than right here in New York by those very persons who accuse philanthropy with seeking to degenerate white blood by an infiltration of colored strains. And the average citizen is voting ships and guns to carry out this programme.

This movement gathered force and strength during the latter half of the nineteenth century and reached its culmination when France, Germany and England and Rus sia began the partition of China and the East. With the sudden self-assertion of Japan its wildest dreams collapsed, but it is still to-day a living, virile, potent force and motive, and the most subtle and dangerous enemy of world peace and the dream of human brotherhood. It has a whole vocabulary of 'its own: the strong races, superior peoples, race preservation, the struggle for survival and a peculiar use of the word "white." And by this it means the right of white men of any kind to club blacks into submission, to make them surrender their wealth and the use of their women, and to submit to the dictation of white men without murmur, for the sake of being swept off the fairest portions of the earth or held there in perpetual serfdom or guardianship. Ignoring the fact that the era of physical struggle for survival has passed away among human beings and that there is plenty of room accessible on earth for all, this theory makes the possession of Krupp guns the main criterion of mental stamina and moral fitness.

Even armed with this morality of the club and every advantage of modern culture, the white races have been unable to possess the earth; many signs of degeneracy have appeared among them; their birthrate is falling, their average ability is not increasing, their physical stamina is impaired, their social condition is not reassuring, and their religion is a growing mass of transparent and self-confessed hypocrisy. Lacking the physical ability to take possession of the world, they are to-day fencing in America, Australia, and South Africa and declaring that no dark race shall occupy or develop the land which they themselves are unable to use. And all this on the plea that their stock is threatened with deterioration from without, when in fact its most dangerous fate is deterioration from within. We are in fact to-day repeating in our intercourse between races all the former evils of class injustice, unequal taxation and rigid caste. Individual nations outgrew these fatal things by breaking down the horizontal barriers between classes. We are bringing them back by seeking to erect vertical barriers between races. Men were told that abolition of compulsory class distinction meant leveling down, degradation, disappearance of culture and genius, and the triumph of the mob. As a matter of fact, it has been the salvation of European civilization. Some deterioration and leveling there was, but it was more than balanced by the discovery of new reservoirs of ability and strength. So to-day we are told that free racial contact—or "social equality" as southern *patois* has it—means contamination of blood and lowering of ability and culture. It need mean nothing of the sort. Abolition of class distinction does not mean universal intermarriage of stocks, but rather the survival of the fittest by peaceful personal and social selection, a selection all the more effective because free democracy and equality of opportunity allow the best to rise to their rightful place.

The same is true in racial contact. The abolition of the lines of vertical race distinction and their tearing away involves fewer chances of degradation and greater opportunities of human betterment than in the case of class lines. On the other hand, the persistence in racial distinctions spells disaster sooner or later. The earth is growing smaller and more accessible. Race contact will become in the future increasingly inevitable, not only in America, Asia and Africa, but even in Europe. The color line will mean not simply a return to the absurdities of class as exhibited in the sixteenth and seventeenth centuries, but even to the caste of ancient days. This, however, the Japanese, the Chinese, the East Indian and the Negroes are going to resent in just such proportion as they gain the power; and they are gaining the power, and they cannot be kept from gaining more power. The price of repression will then be hypocrisy and slavery and blood.

This is the problem of to-day, and what is its mighty answer? It is this great word: The cost of liberty is less than the price of repression. The price of repressing the world's darker races is shown in a moral retrogression and economic waste unparalleled since the age of the African slave trade. What would be the cost of liberty? What would be the cost of giving the great stocks of mankind every reasonable help and incentive to self-development—opening the avenues of opportunity freely, spreading knowledge, suppressing war and cheating, and treating men and women as equals the world over whenever and wherever they attain equality? It would cost something. It would cost something in pride and prejudice, for eventually many a white man would be blacking black men's boots; but this cost we may ignore—its greatest cost would be the new problems of racial intercourse and intermarriage which would come to the front. Freedom and equal opportunity in this respect would inevitably bring some intermarriage of whites and yellows and browns and blacks. If such marriages are proven inadvisable how could they be stopped? Easily. We associate with cats and cows but we do not fear intermarriage with them even though they be given all freedom of development. So, too, intelligent human beings can be trained to breed intelligently without the degradation of such of their fellows as they may not wish to breed with. In the southern United States on the contrary it is assumed that unwise marriage can only be stopped by the degradation of the blacks, the classing of their women with prostitutes, the loading the whole race with every badge of public isolation, degradation and contempt and by burning offenders at the stake.

Is this civilization? No. The civilized method of preventing ill-advised marriage lies in the training of mankind in ethics of sex and childbearing. We cannot ensure the survival of the best blood by the public murder and degradation of unworthy suitors, but we can substitute a civilized human selection of husbands and wives which shall ensure the survival of the fittest. Not the methods of the jungle, not even the careless choices of the drawing room, but the thoughtful selection of the schools and laboratory is the ideal of future marriage. This will cost something in ingenuity, self-control, and toleration but it will cost less than forcible repression.

Not only is the cost of repression to-day large—it is a continually increasing cost, because of the fact that furnished the fatal moral anomaly against which physical slavery could not stand—the free Negro—the Negro who in spite of contempt, discouragement, caste and poverty has put himself on a plane where it is simply impossible to deny that he is by every legitimate measurement the equal of his average white neighbor. The former argument was as I have mentioned that no such class existed. This assertion was persisted in until it became ludicrous. To-day the fashion is come to regard this class as exceptional so far as the logic of the Negro problem is concerned, dangerous so far as social peace is concerned, and its existence more than offset by an abnormal number of criminals, degenerates and defectives.

Right here, then, comes the center of the present problem, namely: What is the *truth* about this? What are the real facts? How far is Negro crime due to inherited and growing viciousness and how far to poverty, degradation and systematic oppression?

How far is Negro labor lazy and how far is it the listless victim of systematic theft?

How far is the Negro woman lewd and how far the helpless victim of social custom?

How far are Negro children being educated to-day in the public schools of the South and how far is the effort to curtail that training increasingly successful?

How far are Negroes leaving the farms and rushing to the cities to escape work and how far to escape slavery?

How far is this race designated as Negroes the descendants of African slaves and how far is it descended from the most efficient white blood of the nation?

What does actual physical and social measurement prove as to the status of these descendants of black men?

All these are fundamental questions. Not a single

valid conclusion as to the future can be absolutely insisted upon without definite skilful scientific answers to these questions and yet not a single systematic effort to answer these questions on an adequate scale has been made in these United States from 1619 to 1909. Not only this but on all sides opposition ranging from indifference and reluctance to actual force is almost universal when any attempt to study the Negro problem adequately is proposed. Yet in spite of this universal and deliberate ignorance the demand is made that one line of solution, which a number of good men have assumed is safe and sane, shall be accepted by everybody and particularly by thinking black men. The penalty for not accepting this programme is to be dubbed a radical, a busy-body, an impatient dreamer and a dangerous agitator. Yet this programme involves justification of disfranchisement, the personal humiliation of Jim-Crowism, a curtailed and purposely limited system of education and a virtual acknowledgment of the inevitable and universal inferiority of black men. And then in the face of this we are asked to look pleasant and do our very best. I think it is the most cowardly dilemma that a strong people ever thrust upon the weak. And I for one have protested and do protest and shall protest that in my humble opinion the assumption is an outrageous falsehood dictated by selfishness, cowardice and greed and for the righteousness of my cause and the proof of my assertions, I appeal to one arbitrament and one alone and that is: THE TRUTH.

THE PROBLEM'S SOLUTION

J. Milton Waldron

President of

The National Negro American Political League

Washington, D. C.

That fearless, able and broad-minded author of "The Negro and the Sunny South"—a book, by the way, every American citizen should read—Samuel Creed Cross, a white man of West Virginia, takes up an entire chapter in his excellent work in giving with the briefest comments even a partial list of the crimes committed by the whites of the South against the Negroes during his recent residence of six months in that section. And last year eighty or ninety colored persons, some of them women and children, were murdered, lynched or burned for "the nameless crime," for murder or suspected murder, for barn burning, for insulting white women and "talking back" to white men, for striking an impudent white lad, for stealing a white boy's lunch and for no crime at all—unless it be a crime for a black man to ask southern men for his rights.

Within the last twelve months Georgia disfranchised her colored citizens by a constitutional subterfuge and Florida attempted the same crime, and almost every white secular newspaper and many of the religious journals of the South contained in every issue of their publications abusive and malicious articles concerning the Negro in which they inflamed the whites against the brother in black and sought to justify the South in robbing him of his labor, his self-respect, his franchise, his liberty and life itself. Many of the officials of southern states, including numerous judges and not a few Christian ministers, helped or sanctioned these Negro-hating editors and reporters in their despicable onslaught upon the Negro, while tens of thousands of business men of the South fattened upon Negro convict and contract labor and the "order system."

Not satisfied with the wrongs and outrages she has heaped upon the colored people in her own borders, the South is industriously preaching her wicked doctrine of Negro inferiority, Negro suppression and Negro oppression in the North, East and West. And yet, in the face of this terrible record of crime against the life, liberty, manhood and political rights of the colored man which is being repeated in the South every day, there are those in high places who have the temerity to tell us that "the Southern people are the Negro's best friends," and that "the Negro problem is a southern problem and that the South should be allowed to solve it in her own way without any interference on the part of the North."

The North and the South together stole the black man from his home in Africa and enslaved him in this land, and this whole nation has reaped the benefits of his two hundred and fifty years of unrequited toil, and the whole nation must see to it that he is fully emancipated, enfranchised, thoroughly educated in heart, head and hand and allowed to exercise his rights as a citizen and earn, wherever and however he can, an honest and sufficient living for himself, his wife and children—this the South cannot do alone and unaided.

Nearly three millions of the ten million Negroes in

this country live north of Mason and Dixon's line and thousands of others are coming North and going West every month; over four hundred thousand of the three millions mentioned above live in Washington, Baltimore, Philadelphia, New York, St. Louis and Chicago; if the Negro problem was ever a southern problem, the colored brother has taken it with him into the North and the West and made it a national problem.

The life, liberty and happiness of the black man and of the white man of this country are so wrapped up together that it is impossible to oppress the one without eventually oppressing the other. The white man of the South was cursed by slavery as much almost as the black man whom he robbed of life, liberty and virtue. In many parts of the South to-day the masses of poor white men are no better off in any sphere of life than the colored people, with the single exception that their faces are white. The rights and liberties of the common people of this entire country have grown less secure, and their ballots have steadily diminished in power since the colored man has been robbed of his franchise by the South; the trusts of the country have seen the rights of millions of loyal black citizens taken from them by the states of the South in open violation of the federal constitution and that with the tacit approval of the highest courts of the land, and they have come to feel that constitutions and laws are not binding upon them, and that the common people—white or black— have no rights which they are bound to respect. The South alone cannot right these gigantic wrongs nor restore to the white people (not to mention the Negroes) in her borders the liberties and privileges guaranteed by the Constitution of the United States.

In discussing the South's attitude towards the colored man we seek only to hold up to scorn and contempt the spirit which predominates in that section; and we desire to condemn only the men of that section who hate their fellow-men, and we wish to bear testimony now and here to the fact that there is an under-current in the South, which is making for righteousness, and that there are a few noble and heroic souls like Rev. Quincy Ewing of Louisiana, and the late Dr. J. L. M. Curry of Virginia, in each southern state who believe that the Negro ought to be treated as a man and given all the rights and privileges accorded any other man. This righteous spirit must, however, be encouraged and strengthened and the number of noble and fair-minded men and women in the South must be greatly augmented, or the battle for human liberty and the manhood and political rights of both races in that section will never be won.

We beg to say that all the enemies of human rights in general, and of the rights of black men in particular, are not in the South; the wrongs complained of by the Negro in that section are, for the most part, the same as those bewailed by the Negro in the North, with this difference: the northern Negro's right to protest against the wrongs heaped upon him is less restricted, and his means of protection and defense are more numerous than those of his southern brother. Already in at least one state north of Mason and Dixon's line Herculean efforts are being put forth to disfranchise the colored man by constitutional enactment; the discrimination against a man on account of his color, and the lynching of Negroes and the burning of their houses by infuriated mobs of white men are not unheard of things in the North and West. Most of the labor unions of these sections are still closed to the brother in black, and most white working men here are determined that the Negro shall not earn a living in any respectable calling if they can prevent it; many of the newspapers North and West (and a few right here in New York City) often use their columns to misrepresent and slander the colored man, and it was only last week when one of the highest courts in the Empire state rendered a decision in which it justified discrimination against a man on the grounds of his color and his condition of servitude. Verily, the Negro problem is not a southern but a national problem.

The most recent solvent proposed for the race problem is the one brought forward by President Taft—which by the way is simply Dr. Washington's prescription revised and amended. Mr. Taft thinks that the Negro problem will be eventually solved if the colored man will make himself useful to the business interests of the community and keep out of sight and out of public office where he is by reason of his numbers or prominence offensive to white people. With regard to the President's solution for the race problem it ought to be said that the reaction in public sentiment in the last twenty years regarding justice to the Negro is as much the result of what is known as the prosperity of the country and the development of its resources as of anything else. In fact, the desire to put the Negro to one side, to segregate him, to assign him to a place at the bottom of the social scheme, has its origin in and receives its support from the dominant commercial and industrial elements of the country. We have been told, and are still told that agitation concerning the Negro hurts business, frightens prosperity and arrests the development of material and commercial resources.

The usual plea now heard in behalf of the Negro and the one which President Taft makes is that his labor is necessary to a section of the country, and that his freedom, his happiness, his morals and his education are to be looked after to the extent that they add to the productiveness and efficiency of his labor and, as a consequence, the enrichment of his employers. It is regarded as good form to refer to the Negro as "an economic asset of the communities where he is found in large numbers," and the idea is spread abroad that whatever decency or consideration is extended to him is for the profit and advantage of others and not for him as a man. While chattel slavery is no longer upheld by the supreme law of the land, the habit and practice in thought and speech of looking at Negroes from the chattel plane still persists. President Taft's advice, if followed, may make slipshod servants of Negroes but it will not train them into good citizens or noble men.

Many solutions for the Negro problem have been proposed, but to our mind there is one and only one practical and effective answer to the question. In the first place we claim that the early friends of the Negro grasped the true solution, which is that his needs and possibilities are the same as those of the other members of the human family; that he must be educated not only for industrial efficiency and for private gain, but to share in the duties and responsibilities of a free democracy; that he must have equality of rights, for his own sake, for the sake of the human race and for the perpetuity of free institutions. America will not have learned the full lesson of her system of human slavery until she realizes that a rigid caste system is inimical to the progress of the human race and to the perpetuity of democratic government.

In the second place, the Negro must make common cause with the working class which to-day is organizing and struggling for better social and economic conditions. The old slave oligarchy maintained its ascendency largely by fixing a gulf between the Negro slave and the white free laborer, and the jealousies and animosities of the slave period have survived to keep apart the Negro and the laboring white man. Powerful influences are at work even to-day to impress upon the

Negro the fact that he must look to the business men of the South alone for protection and recognition of his rights, while at the same time these influences inflame the laboring white man with fears of social equality and race fusion. The Negro, being a laborer, must see that the cause of labor is his cause, that his elevation can be largely achieved by having the sympathy, support and co-operation of that growing organization of working men the world over which is working out the larger problems of human freedom and economic opportunity.

In the third place, wherever in this country the Negro has the franchise, and where by complying with requirements he can regain it, let him exercise it faithfully and constantly, but let him do so as an independent and not as a partisan, for his political salvation in the future depends upon his voting for men and measures, rather than with any particular party.

For two hundred and fifty years the black man of America toiled in the South without pay and without thanks; he cleared her forests, tunneled her mountains, bridged her streams, built her cottages and palaces, cultivated her fields, watered her crops with his tears, fertilized her fields with his blood, nursed her children, protected her women and guarded her homes from the midnight marauder, the devouring flames and approaching disease and death. The colored American willingly and gladly enlisted and fought in every war waged by this country, from the first conflict with the Indians to the last battle in Cuba and the Philippines; when enfranchised he voted the rebellious states back into the Union, and from that day until this he has, as a race, never used his ballot, unless corrupted or intimidated by white men, to the detriment of any part of America. When in power in the South, though for the most part ignorant and just out of slavery and surrounded by vindictive ex-slave owners and mercenary, corrupted and corrupting "carpet baggers," he did what his former masters had failed for centuries to do—he established the free school system, erected asylums for the insane and indigent poor, purged the statute books of disgraceful marriage laws and oppressive and inhuman labor regulations, revised and improved the penal code, and by many other worthy acts proved that the heart of the race was, and is, in the right place, and that whenever the American Negro has been trusted, he has proven himself trustworthy and manly. And when the colored man is educated, and is treated with fairness and justice, and is accorded the rights and privileges which are the birthright of every American citizen, he will show himself a man among men and the race problem will vanish as the mist before the rising sun.

CIVIL AND POLITICAL STATUS OF THE NEGRO

Bishop A. Walters, A. M., D. D.

of

New York City

Through a bloody conflict and the act of the great Lincoln we were emancipated, and later in 1865 we were confirmed in our freedom by the passage of the Thirteenth Amendment to the federal Constitution.

The Fourteenth Amendment, ratified in 1868, made us citizens of the United States and confirmed us in our civil rights. In 1872 the Fifteenth Amendment was ratified which was intended to confirm us in the right of suffrage. We plead for our constitutional rights on the ground that the right of suffrage, when it has been once conferred by the federal government, becomes the inviolable right of every citizen of whatever color, race or rank in social life, and therefore suffrage is not a privilege to be conferred or withheld by the states. The powers of the federal government were not conferred by a single state, but by all the states, therefore, the general government, through congress, can enforce the provisions of the Constitution.

The Negro believes that he should be allowed to retain the franchise in all parts of this land, because of the military service he has rendered the nation. Side by side with his white brother, the Negro has fought bravely in every war of the nation to save the honor of the flag. No one has been more loyal to its colors than he, and he sees no reason why it should not protect him.

He believes that he should be allowed to retain his political rights because he is becoming educated and is being made a strong man; because he is a considerable taxpayer and his wealth is increasing every day. He knows that the cardinal doctrine of this republic is that there shall be no taxation without representation.

The Rev. Frances J. Grimké of Washington, in a recent publication says: "The South does not believe in the civil and political equality of the colored man; does not believe that he should vote, and does not believe that he should hold office. It is not enough that it has deprived us of our civil and political rights within its own territory; it is not enough that within the South itself we have been reduced to a political nonentity, have been placed where the South thinks we belong and where we ought to be kept; but it is now actively engaged in pressing these views upon the whole country. It is working just as zealously now to nationalize its views on the civil and political status of the Negro as it did to nationalize its views on the subject of slavery. Wherever southern men are found, with here and there an exception in northern pulpits, editorial chairs, professorships in colleges and universities, in places of business, they are always actively engaged in propagating this moral and political heresy in regard to the Negro's proper place in the nation, in urging their views upon others." The same argument used to-day was used in the days of slavery to keep the slaves in bondage, but it failed and it will fail again.

Mr. Quincy Ewing, of Louisiana, in an article in the March number of the "Atlantic Monthly," says: "The foundation of the problem, true or false, is the white man's conviction, that the Negro as a race, and as an individual, is his inferior; not human in the sense that he is human, not entitled to the exercise of human rights in the sense that he is entitled to the exercise of them. The problem itself, the essence of it, the heart of it, is the white man's determination to make good this conviction, coupled with constant anxiety lest, by some means, he should fail to make it good. The race problem, in other words, is not that the Negro is what he is in relation to the white man, the white man's inferior; but this, rather: How to keep him what he is in relation to the white man; how to prevent his ever achieving or becoming that which would justify the belief on his part, or on the part of the other people, that he and the white man stand on common human ground."

Says Dr. Grimké: "We are governed but have no part in the government—in the making of laws, in the levying of taxes, in legislation in any shape or form; we are tried and convicted but always, or so nearly always as to make it the rule, by a white jury, by men who from the start are prejudiced against us; we are permitted to testify, but our testimony counts for nothing against the word of a white person. Now the presumption always is, that the white man is innocent until he is proven guilty; the presumption, in case of a colored person, is always that he is guilty until he has proved his innocence, which is well nigh impossible, especially if his accuser happens to be a white person. The disposition always is to accept the statement of the white man against the black man, and never the statement of the black man against the white man. The disposition always is to incriminate the one and to clear the other where there is any conflict between the two."

Now comes the infamous decision of Judge Dugro, of the Supreme Court of New York, who declares that the Negro has no such sensibilities as the white man, forgetting that there are Negroes and Negroes.

"In one sense," says Judge Dugro, "a colored man is just as good as a white man, for the law says he is, but he has not the same amount of injury under all circumstances that a white man would have. Maybe in a colored community down South, where white men were held in great disfavor he might be more injured, but after all in this sort of a community I dare say the amount of evil that would flow to the colored man from a charge like this would not be as great as it probably would be to a white man."

This outrageous decision is followed by the locomotive engineers of Georgia going on a strike to force the Negro firemen from the engines, a position they have held for years. Says the Richmond, Va., "Times-Dispatch:" "It would be easier to sympathize with these striking Georgia railway men if it was felt that their quarrel was reasonable and just, but the reverse seems to be true. The ostensible reason for the strike was the substitution of some Negro fireman for some white firemen, and the presumable reason for these changes was that the Negroes would do the work equally well for less money. A deeper cause for the trouble is suggested by the report that the coming of a certain labor leader from Toronto to Georgia was for the purpose of helping the white firemen to get a raise in pay, a plan which was made difficult or impossible by the presence of the colored firemen.

There is some ground for believing that the race issue has been deliberately emphasized a good deal more than was necessary with a view to enlisting popular support in what is otherwise a simple dispute between capital and labor. But in any case, the root of the trouble appears to lie in the willingness of the Negro to do certain labor for less pay than white men.

Here is a plain economic fact which should be frankly faced. No one can deny that the Negro fireman would like to draw the same pay that goes to the white fireman.

The fact that he has to content himself with less, assuming that he does the work equally well, is an economic discrimination against him on the ground of his color. To insist that the railway pay a higher price than necessary for this work, in order to have it done by a white man, is simply to unionize race prejudice. Unions are supposed to represent all labor, not simply white labor. What they now ask, in effect, is that Negroes shall no longer be employed.

This is the demand which has led to a condition of chaos in Georgia, to the inconvenience of thousands of people. But it must be evident that shoveling coal for an engine is entirely suitable work for a Negro, and that unless he is to be denied all rights, he has a full right to be protected in it. Georgia locomotives have long been stoked by colored firemen. These men have done the work efficiently, and there is no pretense that white engineers object to associating with them in this way. It is all the question of a pay envelope. Georgians who have thoughtlessly sided with the strikers on the appeal to race prejudice, would do well to consider the economic side of this question. If the Negro cannot fire locomotives, what work shall he be allowed to do? Would Georgia rather have her Negroes occupied at hard physical work or loafing around the street corners of Atlanta?"

"The whole trend of this movement among the southern whites," says the "Guardian," "is to keep the Negro down to the same place of social and economic inferiority that he occupied during slavery and restrict them to work as farm laborers, mule drivers, roustabouts, porters, waiters, whitewashers and general utility men."

In view of the foregoing, it is the duty of the members and friends of our race to labor as zealously to change these unfavorable conditions, as the enemy has labored to bring them about. To do this we must first of all determine to make no compromise when manhood rights are involved, and second, as far as possible, the work must be done through organized effort. Everything in our power should be done to encourage the race to continue its intellectual, moral, financial and educational progress. The black man like any other man must so live and act as to command respect as well as to demand it. In the last analysis it is worth that tells.

The need of the hour is the creation of a healthy public sentiment in favor of the enforcement of the Fourteenth and Fifteenth Amendments to the federal Constitution. We should hold public meetings in different sections of the country, and have the best informed men in this and other countries to prepare papers and discuss subjects bearing on this problem. A publication bureau should be organized which should employ first-class writers, black and white, to prepare articles for such magazines as will accept them. In this way we can meet and counteract the insidious attacks which are now being systematically made on the race by those who pretend to be our friends, but who at every turn question our moral, intellectual and financial progress; they take advantage of false criminal statistics in order to change favorable public opinion in the North. We ought to have a lecture bureau, the duty of which should be to secure able and distinguished orators to go up and down the country and to present our cause wherever it is possible to do so.

And, further, I believe that the division of the vote of the black man between the two great parties will greatly aid in the solution of the political problem, especially in the South. The ballot is the badge of political equality, the insignia of one's citizenship, and whenever and wherever there is a disposition on the part of the Democratic party to accept a Negro as an ally and treat him fairly, we should be willing to affiliate with that party.

It is the surest and quickest way to break down political prejudice and have the South permanently recognize our political equality.

We are grateful to President Taft for his expressions of kindness and interest manifested in our welfare, but deeply deplore the impression made upon the South by the question raised in his inaugural address of the expediency of appointment of colored men to office in that section. I am of the opinion that the Negroes of the country are in hearty accord with President Taft in bringing about a closer union between the North and the South, but not at the expense of the black man. I believe them to be in favor of peace between sections, but peace with honor. It is not platitudes we need just now from the President, but the enforcement of the laws which he has sworn to enforce.

LYNCHING OUR NATIONAL CRIME

Mrs. Ida Wells-Barnett

of

Chicago

The lynching record for a quarter of a century merits the thoughtful study of the American people. It presents three salient facts:

First: Lynching is color line murder.

Second: Crimes against women is the excuse, not the cause.

Third: It is a national crime and requires a national remedy.

Proof that lynching follows the color line is to be found in the statistics which have been kept for the past twenty-five years. During the few years preceding this period and while frontier lynch law existed, the executions showed a majority of white victims. Later, however, as law courts and authorized judiciary extended into the far West, lynch law rapidly abated and its white victims became few and far between.

Just as the lynch law régime came to a close in the West, a new mob movement started in the South. This was wholly political, its purpose being to suppress the colored vote by intimidation and murder. Thousands of assassins banded together under the name of Ku Klux Klans, "Midnight Raiders," "Knights of the Golden Circle," etc., spread a reign of terror, by beating, shooting and killing colored people by the thousands. In a few years, the purpose was accomplished and the black vote was suppressed. But mob murder continued.

From 1882, in which year 52 were lynched, down to the present, lynching has been along the color line. Mob murder increased yearly until in 1892 more than 200 victims were lynched and statistics show that 3,284 men, women and children have been put to death in this quarter of a century. During the last ten years from 1899 to 1908 inclusive the number lynched was 959. Of this number 102 were white while the colored victims numbered 857. No other nation, civilized or savage, burns its criminals; only under the stars and stripes is the human holocaust possible. Twenty-eight human beings burned at the stake, one of them a woman and two of them children, is the awful indictment against American civilization—the grewsome tribute which the nation pays to the color line.

Why is mob murder permitted by a Christian nation? What is the cause of this awful slaughter? This question is answered almost daily—always the same shameless falsehood that "Negroes are lynched to protect womanhood." Standing before a Chautauqua assemblage, John Temple Graves, at once champion of lynching and apologist for lynchers, said: "The mob stands to-day as the most potential bulwark between the women of the South and such a carnival of crime as would infuriate the world and precipitate the annihilation of the Negro race." This is the never varying answer of lynchers and their apologists. All know that it is untrue. The cowardly lyncher revels in murder, then seeks to shield himself from public execration by claiming devotion to woman. But truth is mighty and the lynching record discloses the hypocrisy of the lyncher as well as his crime.

The Springfield, Illinois, mob rioted for two days, the

militia of the entire state was called out, two men were lynched, hundreds of people driven from their homes, all because a white woman said a Negro had assaulted her. A mad mob went to the jail, tried to lynch the victim of her charge and, not being able to find him, proceeded to pillage and burn the town and to lynch two innocent men. Later, after the police had found that the woman's charge was false, she published a retraction, the indictment was dismissed and the intended victim discharged. But the lynched victims were dead. Hundreds were homeless and Illinois was disgraced.

As a final and complete refutation of the charge that lynching is occasioned by crimes against women, a partial record of lynchings is cited; 285 persons were lynched for causes as follow:

Unknown cause, 92; no cause, 10; race prejudice, 49; miscegenation, 7; informing, 12; making threats, 11; keeping saloon, 3; practising fraud, 5; practising voodooism, 2; bad reputation, 8; unpopularity, 3; mistaken identity, 5; using improper language, 3; violation of contract, 1; writing insulting letter, 2; eloping, 2; poisoning horse, 1; poisoning well, 2; by white caps, 9; vigilantes, 14; Indians, 1; moonshining, 1; refusing evidence, 2; political causes, 5; disputing, 1; disobeying quarantine regulations, 2; slapping a child, 1; turning state's evidence, 3; protecting a Negro, 1; to prevent giving evidence, 1; knowledge of larceny, 1; writing letter to white woman, 1; asking white woman to marry, 1; jilting girl, 1; having smallpox, 1; concealing criminal, 2; threatening political exposure, 1; self-defense, 6; cruelty, 1; insulting language to woman, 5; quarreling with white man, 2; colonizing Negroes, 1; throwing stones, 1; quarreling, 1; gambling, 1.

Is there a remedy, or will the nation confess that it cannot protect its protectors at home as well as abroad? Various remedies have been suggested to abolish the lynching infamy, but year after year, the butchery of men, women and children continues in spite of plea and protest. Education is suggested as a preventive, but it is as grave a crime to murder an ignorant man as it is a scholar. True, few educated men have been lynched, but the hue and cry once started stops at no bounds, as was clearly shown by the lynchings in Atlanta, and in Springfield, Illinois.

Agitation, though helpful, will not alone stop the crime. Year after year statistics are published, meetings are held, resolutions are adopted and yet lynchings go on. Public sentiment does measurably decrease the sway of mob law, but the irresponsible blood-thirsty criminals who swept through the streets of Springfield, beating an inoffensive law-abiding citizen to death in one part of the town, and in another torturing and shooting to death a man who, for threescore years, had made a reputation for honesty, integrity and sobriety, had raised a family and had accumulated property, was not deterred from its heinous crimes by either education or agitation.

The only certain remedy is an appeal to law. Lawbreakers must be made to know that human life is sacred and that every citizen of this country is first a citizen of the United States and secondly a citizen of the state in which he belongs. This nation must assert itself and defend its federal citizenship at home as well as abroad. The strong arm of the government must reach across state lines whenever unbridled lawlessness defies state laws and must give to the individual citizen under the Stars and Stripes the same measure of protection which it gives to him when he travels in foreign lands.

Federal protection of American citizenship is the remedy for lynching. Foreigners are rarely lynched in America. If, by mistake, one is lynched, the national government quickly pays the damages. The recent agitation in California against the Japanese compelled this nation to recognize that federal power must yet assert itself to protect the nation from the treason of sovereign states. Thousands of American citizens have been put to death and no President has yet raised his hand in effective protest, but a simple insult to a native of Japan was quite sufficient to stir the government at Washington to prevent the threatened wrong. If the government has power to protect a foreigner from insult, certainly it has power to save a citizen's life.

The practical remedy has been more than once suggested in Congress. Senator Gallinger of New Hampshire in a resolution introduced in Congress called for an investigation "with the view of ascertaining whether there is a remedy for lynching which Congress may apply." The Senate Committee has under consideration a bill drawn by A. E. Pillsbury, formerly Attorney-General of Massachusetts, providing for federal prosecution of lynchers in cases where the state fails to protect citizens or foreigners. Both of these resolutions indicate that the attention of the nation has been called to this phase of the lynching question.

As a final word, it would be a beginning in the right direction if this conference can see its way clear to establish a bureau for the investigation and publication of the details of every lynching, so that the public could know that an influential body of citizens has made it a duty to give the widest publicity to the facts in each case; that it will make an effort to secure expressions of opinion all over the country against lynching for the sake of the country's fair name; and lastly, but by no means least, to try to influence the daily papers of the country to refuse to become accessory to mobs either before or after the fact. Several of the greatest riots and most brutal burnt offerings of the mobs have been suggested and incited by the daily papers of the offending community. If the newspaper which suggests lynching in its accounts of an alleged crime, could be held legally as well as morally responsible for reporting that "threats of lynching were heard"; or, "It is feared that if the guilty one is caught, he will be lynched"; or, "There were cries of 'lynch him,' and the only reason the threat was not carried out was because no leader appeared," a long step toward a remedy will have been taken.

In a multitude of counsel there is wisdom. Upon the grave question presented by the slaughter of innocent men, women and children there should be an honest, courageous conference of patriotic, law-abiding citizens anxious to punish crime promptly, impartially and by due process of law, also to make life, liberty, and property secure against mob rule.

Time was when lynching appeared to be sectional, but now it is national—a blight upon our nation, mocking our laws and disgracing our Christianity. "With malice toward none but with charity for all" let us undertake the work of making the "law of the land," effective and supreme upon every foot of American soil —a shield to the innocent and to the guilty punishment swift and sure.

NEGRO DISFRANCHISEMENT AS IT AFFECTS THE WHITE MAN

Hon. Albert E. Pillsbury

Ex-Attorney-General

Massachusetts

The view of Negro disfranchisement and its results which I shall present is not new to many in this audience, but it has never been pressed as it ought to be upon the attention of the country. The indifference with which the people have suffered the process of disfranchisement to go on, without a hand and with hardly a voice raised against it, can be accounted for only upon the belief that they do not understand what it means. I object to it not merely because the Negro is disfranchised in certain states, but because the scheme is a fraud upon the whole country, directly impairing the political rights of every other state, and of every voter in every other state, the white as well as the black.

If it stopped with fraudulent disfranchisement of the Negro, the case would be bad enough, and the public apathy would still be discreditable, though perhaps not unaccountable. It does not stop there. It has multiplied by two or more the political power, in the Federal government, of every white voter in the disfranchising states, and it has to the same extent disfranchised every voter in every other state. It is not merely a question of Negro suffrage, or Negro equality. It is a question of the equality of white men. The question now is whether every white man, in any state, shall be politically the equal of every other white man, in any other state. This question does not belong to any section, but to the whole country. In the face of the claim that Negro suffrage is the affair of the South, with which no other people have any business to interfere, the course of the South has made it the affair of every white citizen in the other thirty-six states who wishes to preserve and defend his own political rights.

Let us first dispose of one or two delusions. They attempt to justify the disfranchisement of the Negro upon various false pretenses, so often repeated and so little denied that they have come to be generally believed. It has been long and loudly asserted that Negro suffrage was forced upon the South. It is not true, and it was never true. The Thirteenth Amendment makes the Negro a freeman, and nothing more. The Fourteenth Amendment makes him a citizen of the United States, with the personal rights of a citizen, and nothing more. The Fifteenth Amendment entitles him to be treated, in respect of the suffrage, only as other men of the same standing or character are treated, and nothing more. The federal law does not make a single Negro a voter, in any state of the Union. The extremest requirement of it is only that the color of his skin shall not disqualify him, if he is otherwise qualified under such laws as any state sees fit to adopt.

Neither is it true that Negro suffrage means Negro control or domination, in any state of the Union. There is not a state in which impartial suffrage, honestly administered, would endanger white supremacy for a day. These two assertions, iterated and reiterated as they have been, and relied upon to justify disfranchisement and reconcile the country to the fraud, are equally and absolutely without foundation.

This is so well known that it cannot be denied. But

when they complain that Negro suffrage was forced upon the South, they will tell you that they mean the forcing of it upon the South by the Reconstruction Acts. Is their case any better here? The Reconstruction Acts did not force Negro suffrage upon the South. They offered restoration to the political rights and privileges forfeited by armed rebellion, on condition that suffrage should be impartial among all citizens of the United States. In view of the penalties which might have been exacted, these terms, unexampled in history for their mildness, do not seem severe. So far as the federal law goes, there has never been a day when any state of the Union could not, by impartial tests applied alike to all citizens, exclude from its suffrage the ignorant, the criminal, the depraved, or even the poor. But the history of the country from 1867 down to this time shows that even these terms, so far as accepted by the white South, were accepted with the fixed purpose to disregard them, so that the Negro should not be allowed to vote. The first experiments in Negro suffrage were met and resisted by armed violence, until it was perceived that fraud is less dangerous and more politic than murder. Then the tissue ballot appeared, and other similar devices. The tissue ballot has now developed into the "grandfather" constitution. Fraud has done its perfect work.

It all comes to this. As a Negro, they like him; indeed they must have him. As a man, a citizen, or a voter, they will have none of him. So far as the suffrage is concerned they have made good this determination, by open disregard and defiance of the Fourteenth and Fifteenth Amendments. This is simply rebellion against the government of the United States, as in 1861, the instrument employed being fraud instead of force. In this, as in all that I say, I refer only to the states where the crime is flagrant, and I acknowledge, with grateful appreciation, the attitude of a minority of the best citizens even in these states, who see the folly and the wickedness of fraudulent disfranchisement of the Negro and have tried to stay its mad career.

While the Fifteenth Amendment gave the Negro nothing but the right to be treated, according to his merits, as other men of equal merit are treated, the white South was even more unwilling to accord him impartial treatment under the Fifteenth Amendment than it was to accept him as a citizen under the Fourteenth, or as a freeman under the Thirteenth. They have nullified, to a substantial extent, all three of the War Amendments. In most of the southern states the Negro has been despoiled, by one sinister device or another, of a substantial share even of the personal liberty supposed to be secured to him by the Thirteenth Amendment. In but few if any of these states is he accorded the privileges of a citizen or the equal protection of the laws, supposed to be secured to him by the Fourteenth Amendment. And now, by a series of fraudulent enactments which began with Mississippi in 1891 and running through and around the "black belt" has finally embraced, actually or practically, every state that seceded from the Union in 1861, the Negro is eliminated from their political system almost as completely as though he did not exist.

That this is a fraud does not need to be asserted. It is self-evident, and is admitted. The disfranchising constitutions, even of the "grandfather" type, are fair enough upon their face, revealing to the eye no open discrimination between the races. So much had to be conceded to the Fifteenth Amendment. But every one of them is calculated, intended and administered, to exclude the Negro from the suffrage, whatever his character and qualifications, while admitting to it every white man, however ignorant, worthless or depraved. It is common knowledge that many of the most distinguished personages concerned in the movement, more candid if less discreet than the rest, have confessed this charge and openly exulted in it.

A new feature has just appeared in the disfranchising process which may be of some significance. We read in the newspapers the other day that the legislature of Florida is proposing to write the word "white" plainly into the constitutional suffrage qualification of that state, openly discarding even the pretense of impartiality between the races which thinly veils the fraud in other states. This looks as though the white South is now confident that the country has abandoned the Negro and that the Fifteenth Amendment may be openly repudiated. The Mississippi senator who appears to be active in the Florida movement probably knows, if the Florida legislature does not, that the Supreme Court has often declared the word "white," if found in the suffrage laws of a state, to be effaced and annulled by the Fifteenth Amendment, of its own force. In view of this, it is difficult to believe that they really expect to do this thing effectively. Whether they think they have discovered a new device, or what the particular purpose is, I do not undertake to say. It may be nothing but a mere piece of bravado, but it needs watching.

Now let us see how disfranchisement of the Negro affects the white man. The Fourteenth Amendment apportions representatives in Congress and presidential electors among the states in proportion to their population, and prescribes that if the suffrage is denied or abridged by a state to any male citizens of the United States of voting age, its representation shall be reduced in the same proportion. At least ten southern states, by fraud or intimidation, under the forms of law or otherwise, have practically or actually disfranchised the Negro. These ten states had by the census of 1900 a population of 15,926,955, of which 9,349,622 are white and 6,565,894 colored. They have 3,675,454 male citizens of voting age, of whom 2,238,720 are white and 1,436,734 colored. The disfranchised colored citizens, a million and a half in round numbers, represent a colored population of six and a half millions. These ten states elect the full number of 82 representatives in Congress, based upon their whole population, and the same number of presidential electors, who represent 2,238,-720 white voters. This is an average of 27,301 voters to each representative and elector. In the other thirty-six states of the Union, 17,122,940 voters elect 309 representatives and presidential electors, an average of 55,-414 voters to each representative and elector. This is more than double the number which exercises the same power in the disfranchising states. A white vote in these states outweighs, in the federal government, two votes of any color in the other states of the Union. A white voter in these states goes to the polls with somewhat more than double the federal power of any voter in the other states.

In fact, the situation is worse than this. The actual voting oligarchy in the disfranchising states is but a small fraction even of the white electorate. I have not attempted to compile any recent figures, but they have often been published. For example, it is said that the congressional vote of a single district in Iowa exceeds the vote which elects the whole congressional delegation of Louisiana; that the average congressional vote in each district in Ohio exceeds the whole congressional vote of Mississippi; and that the vote cast in electing ten congressmen in Wisconsin is more than three times as large as that cast in electing twenty congressmen in South Carolina, Louisiana and Mississippi. Any white voter, in any of the thirty-six states where citizens of the United States are allowed to vote, may figure out for himself, at his leisure, what particular fraction of his own vote the disfranchising states allow him to cast in the choice of the federal government.

One of the sorest spots in the old slave Constitution was the political representation of three-fifths of the slaves, giving the South that undue share of political power. The Fourteenth Amendment was intended to set this right, and to restore and maintain for all time an honest balance of political power between the states. We are now so much worse off than we were then, that whereas but three-fifths of the Negroes were then counted in the basis of representation, the whole are now counted and represented, and the whole political power belonging to about sixteen millions of people is exercised by a white electorate representing about nine millions. Instead of carrying us forward to political equality, the actual results of the war have carried us backward to more inequality.

All this has been done in plain and open disregard and violation of the Fourteenth and Fifteenth Amendments. It has passed into a political truism that the three amendments of the Constitution were the whole fruits of the war. We have suffered ourselves to be robbed of the fruits, by a new rebellion against the federal government, in which the states of the late Confederacy have taken and hold more political power than they formerly had by virtue of slavery itself. In the recent bill of Congressman Bennet, of New York, to enforce the representation clause of the Fourteenth Amendment, based upon the figures of the census of 1900, it appears that the ten disfranchising states there dealt with, now represented on the basis of the whole population by 82 congressmen and the same number of electors, are entitled to but 50 congressmen and electors, and that 32 representatives and electors of these states are now voting in Congress and in the election of president and vice-president without right, and in open violation of the federal Constitution.

It was long hoped, and perhaps believed, that the judicial remedy for disfranchisement in violation of the Fifteenth Amendment would be effective. One mistaken view of the judicial remedy has obtained some currency and ought to be corrected. Mr. Blaine seems to have thought, when he wrote his Twenty Years of Congress, that it must be the only remedy. He there expressed the view that the Fifteenth Amendment, directly forbidding discrimination against the Negro in the suffrage, superseded the representation clause of the Fourteenth which appears to permit it at the price of reduced representation; that as the Fifteenth wholly forbids denial of the suffrage on the ground of color, a state can no longer deny it, or be found or held to have denied it, on that ground; and that the only thing to be done upon violation of the Fifteenth Amendment is to appeal to the courts. In this he was plainly wrong, and his view has not been and is not to be accepted. The Fourteenth Amendment is not a permission to the states to deny the suffrage to any class of citizens. Suffrage, in general, is the affair of the states. They need no permission of the federal government to regulate it. This Amendment says to the states: If the Negro is not admitted to the suffrage, the Negro shall not be counted in the basis of representation. The Fifteenth Amendment says to the states: While you may regulate the suffrage to suit yourselves, you shall not deny it to the Negro merely because he is a Negro. This does not supersede the other provision, first, because there is no inconsistency between the two, the later being cumulative and supplemental, not repugnant, to the other; second, because to forbid an act does not repeal a penalty otherwise laid upon it; and third, because the judicial remedy, under the Fifteenth Amendment, may be sought by

187

any aggrieved citizen, and perhaps only by a citizen, while the remedy by reduction of representation, under the Fourteenth Amendment, is a public remedy, enforceable only by Congress, which the additional private remedy under the Fifteenth cannot be held to supersede or disturb.

And further, Congress is expressly empowered to enforce the Fifteenth Amendment, by "appropriate" legislation. No legislation can be more appropriate than to reduce the representation of a disfranchising state, in pursuance of the plain mandate of the Fourteenth Amendment that its representation "shall be reduced" in such a case. In framing the Fifteenth Amendment, it may have been foreseen, as the case has actually turned out to be, that the suffrage might be denied or abridged by some device which could not be brought to the judicial test, or that the court might hold the political remedy to be exclusive. It may be, in theory, that a state is incapable of doing what the federal Constitution forbids it to do, so that, abstractly, a state cannot now deny or be found to have denied the suffrage on the sole ground of color, as the attempt to do it is legally void. But this is mere casuistry. The law knows no such refinement as to assume that a forbidden act cannot be done because it is forbidden. Such an assumption would nullify all penal legislation. It is common knowledge that acts forbidden by law are done, and punished, every day. The Amendments deal with facts, not theories, and Congress may deal with the facts, as it finds them to be.

The two Amendments must be read together. Taken together, they mean that a state shall not deny the suffrage to any citizen of the United States on the sole ground of race, color or previous servitude, but if actually denied, upon this or any other ground, it shall be at the cost of reduced representation.

It is now familiar that the Supreme Court, in the few

cases which have reached it, has avoided the direct question of the conflict of the disfranchising constitutions with the Fifteenth Amendment. The scheme is so cunningly contrived as to make it difficult or impossible to present an effective case. The court has not yet been squarely faced with the main question, and has plainly shown a reluctance to meet it. The nearest approach was in the Alabama case,* in 1903, where the subject is briefly surveyed, and a majority of the judges declares the court incompetent to give the desired relief. If this declaration was extra-judicial, as it may be regarded, it is perhaps the more significant for that reason, whatever may be said of its propriety. In this and other cases the judges must have perceived that if the question is forced upon the court, the result will be either to sustain a patent and colossal political fraud, or to overturn the suffrage systems of states by judicial decree. Rightly or wrongly, they shrink from this alternative. I think that the Alabama case must be taken as a final refusal to pass upon the general validity of the disfranchising constitutions if the question can possibly be avoided.

But this is not the whole of the Alabama case. The court concludes with a pregnant declaration that relief from such a political wrong, done by a state or its people, must·be given by them, "or by the legislative and political department of the government of the United States." That there is a complete political remedy must have been apparent to the court, and it cannot be without significance that the court points directly to the political remedy, in turning away from the subject.

While the judicial remedy for disfranchisement has thus far proved delusive, there is complete power in Congress and the Executive to enforce political equality

*Giles v. Harris, 189 U. S. 475.

among the citizens of the United States if disposed to enforce it, and this not merely under the Fourteenth but under Section 2 of the Fifteenth Amendment itself, which declares, as in the other war Amendments, that "the Congress shall have power to enforce this Article by appropriate legislation."

This clause of the Amendment is of the same force and significance as the prohibitive clause. Plainly the Constitution has not left its enforcement to the courts. Congress has express power to "enforce" its provisions, by "appropriate" legislation. This must be held a plenary and effective power, adequate to the complete enforcement of the prohibition of the first section. What is "appropriate" legislation for this purpose? I have suggested one example of it. We have some further light upon this question. In the Civil Rights cases, and others, the court has held that the similar section of the Fourteenth Amendment does not authorize Congress to substitute for unconstitutional laws of a state a new code, of its own making, but only to enact "corrective legislation, that is, such as may be necessary and proper for counteracting such laws as the states may adopt or enforce, which, by the Amendment, they are prohibited from making or enforcing, or such acts and proceedings as the states may commit or take, which, by the Amendment, they are prohibited from committing or taking."

Granting that Congress may not directly enact that the Negro shall be allowed to vote in any state, under this power as thus expounded it may at least declare void, for all federal purposes, any provisions of a state law or constitution which it finds to be in violation of the Amendment. The power is a legislative power, to be exercised by legislation. A legislative body proceeds upon facts found or ascertained by itself, to its own satisfaction. It needs no other authority for its action, and if it acts within its constitutional authority, the facts upon which it proceeds cannot be questioned or its action disturbed. All this must be taken as known and intended in conferring the power. An Act of Congress declaring a law or system of laws, so far as it affects the federal government, to be void for violation of the Amendment, is not constructive but is strictly corrective legislation. It would at once furnish sufficient ground for the House of Representatives to purge itself of members who have no right to be there. It would be the plain duty of the House, notwithstanding it is subject to no control in dealing with its membership, to exclude members elected under a suffrage system found and declared by Congress to be void for violation of the federal Constitution. It would equally be the duty of the two Houses to refuse to count the votes of presidential electors chosen under such a system. This proceeding would compel reformation of the suffrage system of the disfranchising states, under the alternative of possible loss of their whole representation in the lower House of Congress and in the electoral body. Probably it has never been expected that the courage of Congress would rise to this level unless under the stress of some future political exigency, when it might again be found that there is "politics" in the Negro. But there is always politics in the white man, and this is a white man's issue, to be pressed upon the government by white men. Here is a plain remedy, in the hands of Congress. If applied, it cannot justly be complained of. If not applied, every voter in thirty-six states has a right to complain. It goes directly to the end which the Fifteenth Amendment was intended to secure. It does not by any means exhaust the political remedies under this Amendment, but it is enough to suggest the possibilities of the enforcement clause, and to show how formidable a weapon is here placed in the hands of Congress to restore political equality among the citizens of the United States.

Section 2 of the Fourteenth Amendment, the representation clause, is more familiar, but even this has not been fully explored. It declares that if the right to vote is denied "or in any way abridged," except for rebellion or other crime, the basis of representation "shall be reduced" in the same proportion. The penalty is not limited to direct denial of the suffrage. The clause "or in any way abridged" is no less significant and effective than the other. Not merely "denied," not merely "abridged," but for further and complete assurance, "*in any way* abridged," is the law. No secret, covert or sinister scheme, however cunningly contrived, by which abridgement may be effected without direct denial, shall prevail. Nothing could meet the "grandfather" device, or the "understanding" device, more directly than this. It seems as though the framers of the Amendment, with prophetic foresight, had anticipated what now has actually been done, and fitted the Amendment to the facts. Adroitly as the disfranchising constitutions have avoided direct denial of the suffrage to the Negro, it can avail them nothing. Neither court nor Congress could hesitate in finding that the suffrage is abridged to the Negro in the administration of the system, if not directly denied by its terms, and this is violation of the Amendment.

Under this clause there is a complete remedy for disfranchisement in the hands of the House of Representatives by itself. It is not prescribed that *Congress may* reduce the representation of a disfranchising state. Upon denial or abridgement of the suffrage, its representation "shall be reduced." It is judicially declared and settled that the War Amendments are intended to be, and are, of automatic action and self-executing, so far as they can be without the aid of legislation. A plain and conceded purpose of this section is to correct the inequality of the old Constitution by excluding from the basis of representation any part of the population which is not represented in the electorate; in short, to forbid and prevent any representation of any state not based upon a voting population, the states having the choice to confer the suffrage and have the representation or withhold the suffrage and lose it.

Read in its full meaning, the Amendment prescribes that if a state withholds the suffrage from any class of citizens of the United States its representation shall thereby stand as reduced, *ipso facto,* in the same proportion. A proportionate part of its right to representation ceases to exist, contemporaneously with denial or abridgment of the suffrage, and from that moment it has no constitutional right to send any representatives to Congress. or choose any presidential electors, except such number as may stand upon the reduced basis. Upon finding of the fact of denial or abridgment of the suffrage, the proportionate reduction of representation follows as a necessary consequence. The House of Representatives may find this fact, and deal with representation accordingly, without any concurrent action of the Senate or the Executive.

Every representative sent from a disfranchising state since the disfranchising process began, in excess of this reduced number, has been sent without authority, and has occupied his seat without right or title. The House of Representatives would have been legally warranted, at any time since Mississippi disfranchised the Negro in 1891, in refusing to admit any delegation from a disfranchising state. When such a delegation appears, it is known that its number exceeds the number which the state has a constitutional right to send, and as they all stand upon the same ground and are alike subject to the same infirmity, the House cannot distinguish between them and is not called upon to admit either or any of them. It is for any state to make the title of each of its representatives good, by sending only such number as the Constitution authorizes. A suffrage system in violation of the federal Constitution is, so far as it affects the federal government, void as an entirety, and no representative claiming to be elected under such a system can show a constitutional title to a seat in Congress.

It has heretofore been assumed that reduction of representation under the Fourteenth Amendment can be effected only by an Act of Congress in the form of which Congressman Bennet's bill is the latest example, declaring the number of representatives which each disfranchising state is entitled to elect, and requiring the state to reconstruct its districts accordingly or to elect at large the proper number and no more. While this method of procedure is preferable, especially as it conclusively settles the title of the state to presidential electors no less than to representatives, it is not legally necessary. The House of Representatives has power enough in its own hands.

If these remedies for disfranchisement appear extreme, it is only because the people of the country at large, in their indifference to the fate of the Negro, have overlooked the crime against their own political rights. They are directly within the terms and intent of the Constitution, they are essential to the supremacy of the federal power, they are demanded in order to restore political equality among all the states and all citizens of the United States, and it is the plain duty of the government to apply them. If the power is doubted, as the Supreme Court once said in a similar case, "it is only because the Congress, through long habit and long years of forbearance has, in deference and respect to the states, refrained from the exercise of these powers, that they are now doubted." Action of Congress in this direction, or even a near prospect of it, would bring the disfranchising states to a realizing sense of the danger involved in their open defiance of the organic law. The men who shaped the War Amendments, and the people who wrote them into the federal charter, could not have conceived that there should ever be any hesitation to enforce them under such conditions as now confront us.

The application of this remedy will at least restore political equality among the states and among the white citizens of the United States, and it will not stop here. It will accomplish what the Fourteenth Amendment was designed to accomplish, by establishing impartial suffrage and equality of political rights among all citizens of the United States without distinction based upon race or color. No state will willingly pay the price of reduced representation for the luxury of depriving all Negroes of the ballot. So long as ten states are allowed, without interference or remonstrance, to enjoy this privilege and at the same time to retain and exercise all the political power of which the disfranchised Negroes are despoiled, they can hardly be expected to surrender it. So long as we remain dumb and subservient, we cannot hold them alone responsible for the consequences.

Here is a plain question, which ought to be put to the country and answered by the country. Are the people of thirty-six states willing to be defrauded of their own political rights in order that ten states may disfranchise the Negro? Have we so fallen from the estate of our fathers that, while they vigorously remonstrated against lawful representation of three-fifths of the Negroes, sanctioned by the Constitution, we will submit to unlawful representation of all the Negroes in defiance of the Constitution? This question, once fairly presented, cannot be put aside until it is settled, and it will not be settled until the political rights of every citizen of the United States are recognized and enforced.

The effective nullification of the Fifteenth Amendment is now followed by a concerted movement to prepare the public mind for its formal abrogation. If

such a movement can succeed, it will not stop with
the Fifteenth Amendment, but the representation clause
of the Fourteenth will be the next object of attack.
With both of these clauses of the Constitution out of
the way, they will have the Negro where they want to
put him, and they will have us where they want to put
us. The president takes notice of this in his inaugural
address, where he declares that the Fifteenth Amendment
will never be repealed, and that it ought to be "observed."
It ought to be enforced. Until enforced it is virtually
repealed. It is a part of his official duty to see that it
is enforced. Will he do it? He owes the people of the
United States an answer to this question. The people
owe it to themselves to see that it is answered, and there
is but one possible answer.

It is not the part of patriotism or of statesmanship
to trifle with this subject. If the organization and control of the House of Representatives should turn upon
the thirty-odd votes now unlawfully retained by the
white South, the subject would be precipitated into politics in a day, not as a question of principle, or for the
assertion of any principle, but upon the lowest level, as
a means of perpetuating the power of the dominant party. If a presidential election should turn
upon the thirty-odd electoral votes now under the
same unlawful control, there would be a struggle for
possession of the government to which tne contest of
1876 was but a passing breeze. Out of this issue, if
forced upon us under such conditions, a storm may
arise which will shake the federal structure to its foundations. It is a plain duty to press the subject upon the
attention of the country until public sentiment compels
the government to act. If deaf to the disfranchised
Negro it will hear the disfranchised white man, and the
act which takes care of the white man will take care of
the Negro.

THE NEED OF ORGANIZATION

Mr. Oswald Garrison Villard

of

New York

I beg to report on behalf of your committee on organization that it has seemed from the very inception of this movement desirable that some permanent body should grow out of this gathering. Hence your committee has found no difficulty in deciding that these conferences at least should become annual events. When music teachers, dancing masters, commercial travellers, secret orders galore, and associations of college graduates find it worth their while to meet annually; when the annual arbitration meetings and conferences on the status of the North American Indian at Mohonk have so clearly demonstrated their value, it seems perfectly obvious that those men and women who believe that the welfare of the republic is bound up with fair play towards the Negro, with giving him exact justice and exact equality before the law, should come together once every twelve months for encouragement, for information, for inspiration. Your committee recommends, therefore, that there be appointed by the Chair a committee of not more than thirty persons who shall be charged with the duty of calling the conference together in 1910 and with forming a permanent organization which shall have still further and vastly more important duties. Your committee bespeaks your approval of its plan to bring about the establishment of a permanent, incorporated national committee, to forward the interests of the Negro and to combat race prejudice in the United States. In explanation of this proposal, I beg leave to say a few words.

"The timidity of our public opinion is our disease, or, shall I say the publicness of opinion, the absence of private opinion," Emerson once declared. No one who is to-day interested in the progress upwards of the colored race, the maintenance intact of all its rights and privileges, can dispute the evident application of these words to latter-day conditions. There is getting to be an absence of private opinion on questions concerning colored men and women in certain circles of the North, which in itself makes clear the undertaking of a systematic effort to place the facts in regard to our colored citizens before the American nation. In the absence of an enlightened individual opinion, it is easy enough for the multitude to accept for truisms certain allegations in regard to colored people which float up to us from the South or have their origin in equally prejudiced quarters in the North. For race prejudice knows no geographical distinctions; it is hemmed in no more by Mason and Dixon's line than was slavery successfully curtailed by the Missouri Compromise of 1820. It was always to be found in the North in slavery days—was not Prudence Crandall's school for colored children burned in Connecticut in 1834?—precisely as it is to be found in Prussia, Russia, and Austria to-day, though along other lines than those in which it manifests itself in our own country. Of late, with us, there is every evidence that a systematic effort is being made to win over to the exact view of the South the bulk of northern opinion. Senator Tillman of South Carolina did us the very great service the other day of setting forth in the frankest of language the southern programme at the dinner of the

South Carolina society, in this city. "At the same time," he said, "I want to speak of the great change that has come over the North in the last few years. One reason for this is that the old abolitionists are dying out, and we only find the agitator in some old soldier, who is drawing a pension he never earned, and who never saw a Confederate soldier, but who has of late years become a great warrior. Fifteen years after the North tried to pass a force bill to let Negroes vote, the President of the United States declares that he will not appoint an officer to the government service who is obnoxious to us.

"They say we must enforce the laws impartially, and we say we will not. We have nullified the Fourteenth Amendment, and in every southern state the Negro is disfranchised. We hear much about the 'grandfather clause' in our voting qualification. The reason we put that in is to give the poor white men who cannot read a chance to vote and to disfranchise the Negro.

"The Negro to-day is a Republican asset. He holds the balance of power in Philadelphia, and in Ohio, Indiana, and Illinois. And so long as the Republicans continue to use him as a political asset it is our duty to be true to the civilization of our fathers and to educate the North, as we have been doing during the last ten years."

Now, if there were no other reason than this speech of Senator Tillman for calling this conference, that would be enough. It affords in itself plenty of reason for beginning a scientifically planned and aggressive movement on behalf of the Negro's rights even if there were no such words in our language as justice, equality, fair play, and national good faith.

The enlightened traveller who comes to this country from Europe, whether it be Dr. Barth from Germany, or H. G. Wells or Sir Harry Johnston from England, to study our social and racial conditions, is usually appalled at the prejudice against the Negro he encounters. The thoughful foreigner soon asks what self-defence organizations the colored people and their white sympathizers have formed. Where, he asks, is your national steering committee, like those that have constituted themselves in Europe to watch over and guard the interests of the Jewish race? He learns that there is none. "What," he says, "have you no group of national leaders, like those which have for decades fought the battles of the Irish people in and out of Parliament?" Again the answer must be no. "Surely," he gasps, "there is some militant committee, like that of the Prussian Poles, which has thus far successfully defeated the efforts of the Prussian government to make its Polish subjects abandon their language, their customs, yes, even their lands?" Again the reply must be in the negative. Our puzzled foreign friend may next ask about the educational status of the Negroes. He learns that Congress grants no federal aid of any consequence, and that it does not interfere with the laws of any state in regard to public education. So he asks: "Of course, there is some national organization which deals solely with Negro education?" To this the only reply that can be given is that there are several funds which contribute more or less—mostly less—to colored schools, but the problem has never been approached in a thoroughgoing, systematic, or scientific way; that in the main the schools specially founded to aid the colored people rely upon haphazard contributions from a generous public. As a result, they are without proper guidance or supervision, and there flourish side by side with effective institutions ineffective ones, and even some which exist solely for the salaries they pay to teachers.

When our foreigner has finished wondering at this state of affairs his next question is for the name of that militant organization which battles incessantly for the civil and political rights of the Negro. Here his informant is not quite as much at loss, for there exists, among other useful societies, the Constitution League that has so manfully fought the battle of the shamefully ill-treated Brownsville soldiers and is seeking to obtain from the Supreme Court of the United States decisions which shall fortify the Negro in his right. There is the admirable Niagara movement; but even this and the similar organizations have not yet established a legal aid bureau. One of the best and most useful philanthropies in New York City is the Legal Aid Society, which gives free legal advice and aid to the poor. If this work has demonstrated its usefulness in a city, would it not be a thousandfold more useful when applied to a race? More than that, the inhabitants of the teeming East and West Sides of New York do not begin to need legal protection as do the Negroes of the South, and at times those of the North. We do not hear of any blind member of our local foreign population being tied up and flogged with a rawhide whip to make him confess; we have not yet heard of any man's being lynched in Essex Street because someone accused him of a heinous crime. We have never heard of New Yorkers being run out of town, their lives endangered, their families abused, their property destroyed, merely because they happened to be considered too prosperous, too well-to-do, to suit their neighbors of another race. But it is not necessary to enumerate the thousand and one crimes against colored people, nor to remind this assembly that a Negro in the South is never tried by his peers, but always by a jury that consists of men whose consciousness of their superiority would rouse them to bitter anger if any one remarked that they were but the equals of the prisoner at the bar. Never has a race needed more a strong central legal bureau able to employ the ablest counsel to prosecute men who kill and call it law; ever ready to insist upon the punishment of guilty officials, and to cure the lynching evil by prosecuting lax authorities and bringing civil suits for damages against the local or county authorities.

Realizing to the full the justice of the criticisms of the foreigners who come to us, your committee, whose interest in the colored race is nothing new, but is based upon experience and study of years therefore believes that the time has come for a committee or a board or a limited society which shall do for the colored people what the Zionist committees do for the Jews; what the Prussian Polish Committee has done for the Poles, and the Irish committees for their wronged people. This board should have a national charter and be regularly incorporated so as to be perpetual and to be able to seek and to receive large amounts of money by donations or bequests. If there ever was a case where millions should be given it is this one; and your committee believes that if such a board should be well established and well-manned it would have no difficulty in raising, in time, large sums. The colored people would contribute just as soon as convinced, first, of the sincerity and unselfishness of the enterprise; second, of its absolute independence of any of the factions within the race; third, that it was on a scientific and an efficient basis, and fourth, that it was wedded to no particular form of education, but to all forms of education. Mr. Richard R. Wright, jr., estimates that the Negroes of the United States have paid in direct property and poll taxes for schools no less than $45,000,000 during the last forty years, besides $15,-000,000 through their churches. It is not leaving the realm of the credible, therefore, to believe that they could be got to contribute large sums to the endowment of the national board proposed.

It would be difficult in the time allotted to me to enumerate all the beneficent possibilities of such a board, but there could be no more important duty for it than to spread the truth about the colored people. Every lynching should be investigated by a competent committee; every injustice to the Negro should spread throughout the press; the marvellous achievements of the colored people set forth in their true colors, and above all a campaign of education of the white people carried on. One of the foremost leaders of the new movement for education in the South stated privately the other day that if he had a million dollars he would devote it to the education of the educated white people of the South, and it is a most encouraging fact that in this undertaking he would have the aid of a growing number of white people, who have seen the light—men like former Congressman Fleming of Georgia, Prof. John Spencer Bassett, President Denny of Washington and Lee University, the Rev. Quincy Ewing of Louisiana, and many others whose writings should go into every household of the South. The publicity bureau of this board should then comprise a research section to carry on the work of the kind so admirably done under Dr. Du Bois's direction, at Atlanta University, and in co-operation therewith a press section in charge of an accomplished newspaper man.

The political and civil rights bureau of our national board would naturally be its most important undertaking, for it would bend its energies to bringing about the enforcement of the Fourteenth and Fifteenth Amendments, to obtaining court decisions upon the disfranchising laws and other discriminatory legislation. For this purpose it should have at its disposal sufficient money to employ the highest legal talent obtainable and to pay the heavy cost of carrying up to the Supreme Court case after case until that shifting and evasive body is compelled to decide whether there shall be two degrees of citizenship in this country, whether there shall be separate laws for one class of human beings and others for different human beings; whether special privilege in its most obnoxious form shall have legal sanction, and whether the Constitution of the United States shall be permanently violated. A non-partisan body like our proposed board could often do this with greater effectiveness than any organization of voters as such, for it would in no wise enter the political field for the purpose of electing this or that candidate, but confine itself battling for principles, for civic rights, for an untarnished Constitution.

The education bureau of our board would find a broad field in uplifting the standards of Negro schools and colleges, in improving their business methods, devising less wasteful plans of raising funds, and, if sufficiently equipped, in making donations to worthy institutions of all classes. Our proposed industrial bureau should deal with the colored man in relation to labor; it might take over in this city the functions of that excellent body which seeks to create additional industrial opportunities for colored workers, and could found and aid similar societies in other industrial centres. It could concern itself with the whole question of housing and of land owning, both urban and rural, and could, if it were deemed advisable, make large purchases of land for re-sales to colored people. In the possession of land lie enormous strength and defensive power. The Poles in Prussia, owing to their enormous land holdings, have successfully defied every effort of the government they hate to Prussianize them until that tyrannical government has found itself compelled, as a last resort, to deprive them by force of their land holdings. There is surely a lesson in this that we cannot too rapidly acquire land for colored farmers and workers in all sections of our country. The question of emigration, of moving large bodies of colored people from one section to another, is another one with which a national board might well concern itself, for therein, too, lies a weapon of great usefulness in the compelling of justice.

To mention only one more function of our proposed board, it should be equipped to aid the individual colored man of merit, as well as a meritorious community, by giving him the best education possible and then placing him where he can be of the greatest service to his people. We see too many colored physicians in the cities and too few in the rural districts; there are too many Negroes capable of earning $5,000 a year at $2,000 jobs. Where a splendid intellect is discovered, we want to set it tasks that will make it worth one hundred cents on the dollar to both races of this country, and not confine it to duties which a $1,200 man can perform just as well.

In other words, in this era of organized publicity and of combinations of capital and brains in every field of human endeavor your committee believes that the white friends of the Negro and the Negro himself should fall in line with the times and use the very best tools for his defence and his advancement. Never was it truer that there is strength in union; never was it plainer that the emergency demanded the most efficient means of appealing to the conscience and the hearts of the American people. At heart the great masses are sound on every question—if one can but get the facts before them. What would have seemed more hopeless than an attempt to stir the national conscience at the time of the founding of the "Liberator"? Is not to-day every great crusade, whether on behalf of child labor, the conservation of our national resources, or the warfare on tuberculosis, conducted on precisely these lines suggested—with a publicity bureau and a national committee? If our plan seems a counsel of perfection, let us in truth hitch our wagon to a star and devote our lives, if necessary, to its realization. Some of us are willing to give freely of our strength and our time to it, because we are convinced that its infinite possibilities of usefulness to our country will be limited only by its finances, and that alliance with such a board would mean patriotic service of the highest degree to all our people, white or black or yellow. With this feeling we ask the adoption of our resolution and your support for our great project. We are happy to add that two of the most useful of the political organizations fighting for the Negroes' rights are ready to co-operate with or coalesce with our proposed board, whichever seems best. They are ready to join us in creating a body which shall bring home to the heart of every man whom it can reach the existence of gross injustice and oppression in this land of the free and home of the brave and shall never let the nation forget that it has a vital, pressing race-problem on its hands until that problem is settled in consonance with the principles of an exact justice.

EFFECT ON POOR WHITES OF DISCRIMINATION AGAINST NEGROES

Hon. Joseph C. Manning

of

Alabama

Growing out of the attitude of the controling element in the South towards the Negro, as a consequence of the ingenious exploitation of the race problem there is no constitutional or free government in any immediate southern state. There is not a state in the group of the far southern states that is not dominated by a brutal political minority of the whites, without mention of the suppression of all blacks.

This political savagery is clamped together by intrigue and cunning. It holds sway through written and unwritten processes made possible by as artful a system of strategy as could find crafty conveyance in forms of state constitutional law. These compacts, these state oligarchies, are absolutely without any political moral cohesive force to hold them together. It is necessary, therefore, to make secure their domination that this régime should not only beat down and oppress all blacks, but should extend this system of exploitation until it submerges the liberties of a majority of whites.

The next census will no doubt show that there are 300,000 whites of voting age in Alabama. It will show the number of Negroes of over 21 years of age, males, to be about 200,000. As a result of the operations, of the swing of the Bourbon axe, as an outcome of the machinations of the oligarchy, the election year of 1910 will disclose the fact that the whole number of whites in Alabama out of the voting—who do not and who can not vote, by reason of the workings and aggressions of our peculiar southern political institutions—will equal the entire number of male blacks of voting age.

This· condition is ingeniously explained away by the degenerate statesmanship of the South and is now very readily accepted by the duped political leadership of the North as wholly necessary to uphold white supremacy; whereas these régimes have swept away and submerged the political rights of whites just as brutally as they have pressed this iron heel of political despotism on all blacks.

Those most responsible for this situation are of the same flesh, the same families, the same sentiments as what is known in our southern history as the slave owning political and social aristocracy. This régime dominating Alabama now is simply the progeny of the old slave-owning oligarchy. The attitude of these men to the Negro is no unknown thing to the nation, but the astounding way in which this aggression has been permitted to march forward in its brutal political despotism is not comprehended, in all its various and vicious aspects.

These men who, by reason of their being born and bred into antipathy to the Negro, do not hesitate to withhold from him the political rights which the American Constitution says that he is entitled to are not so pure in heart and so unselfish and lofty in ideal as to be worthy to have committed to their exclusive keeping either the hopes and future of all blacks or the absolute, ring-riveted, intrigue-entrenched control of this vast majority of politically helpless whites.

It is not strange, it is only what might be expected to follow as a result of our southern political leadership, that we have a vast illiterate and impoverished white population. It will be remembered that some southern representatives in Congress did not warm up to the Blair bill for national aid to education. The inference they caused to be drawn by their constituents was that it was because of the Negro, but there is now a well founded opinion these leaders of this oligarchy felt themselves a bit more secure in political power without an educated, thinking, independent white constituency. These men have felt capable of subduing the blacks, but the problem with them, that with which they have had to deal in these recent years, is the suppression of the revolting masses of the whites.

That these men are masters of the situation the existing conditions thoroughly demonstrate. It is to-day as impossible for the opposition majority of whites, without including the blacks, to overthrow this political despotism of the minority in the state of Alabama as was it impossible for the Negro in that state to free himself from the manacles and chains of chattel slavery in 1860. This cruel and unjust system, interwoven to-day as it was before the civil war in all social and political affairs, is bolstered up by an intolerance that has to many the fierceness of the very jaws of hell and constitutes a social and political barbarity as heartlessly disregardful of whites who oppose it as were the old slave holders heartless to freedom's cry for enslaved blacks.

That treacherous cry of "let the South alone" is as ungodly, as infamous to-day as was that anti-abolition and copperhead sentiment of the North detestable in 1860. Any man, whoever he may be, however exalted may be his station, who palliates, excuses, or knowingly and willingly acquiesces in the aggressions of this system which now insidiously seeks extension of its influence and power into the free states of the North, is, whether he so wills it or not, aiding and abetting a clique in these states of the South, who are at this hour as much in revolt against the letter and the spirit of the amendments to the American Constitution as they were out of the Union when they trained the guns of their Confederacy at the flag of this Republic.

THE NEGRO AND THE NATION

Dr. William A. Sinclair

of

Philadelphia

That the nation should remain apathetic, supine, limp; seemingly dazed in the presence of this frenzied, dashing, over-weening, over-bearing, over-reaching, imperialistic southern leadership, is not a new thing under the sun. It was even so in the days of slavery. The nation temporized and procrastinated with slavery until the monster all but stung it to death. Is the lesson so soon forgotten? Has the tremendous cost ceased even to be a dream?

I may assert that the nation is, even now, in the midst of the gravest complications. Already southern leadership has inaugurated a condition of semi-slavery in the southern states. The situation is growing alarmingly worse. He that runs may read. And this explosive situation is being tempered with high sounding phrases about the fraternal relations between the sections, the obliteration of all sectional lines, the accord and concord between the North and South. I say, solemnly and deliberately, that all this talk and palaver is the merest twaddle. It is without foundation in reason or in fact.

There can be no real obliteration of section lines, no genuine spirit of fraternity, no bona fide concord between the sections, so long as southern leadership draws its inspiration and takes its cue from the brutal traditions of slavery, and disregards the dictates of humanity and justice, and tramples under foot the laws of God and the laws of the republic in dealing with their fellow man, thus putting "the South once more in a position provokingly offensive to the moral sense and the enlightened spirit of the world outside."

Among those of responsibility and great prestige who have made deliverances on this question, I may refer to President Taft. Mr. Taft has repeatedly gone out of his way, both by words and by deeds to placate the South. The people of the North trust him, not because they believe that he is always wise in these matters, but because they believe that he is always honest.

Mr. Taft, while he was a candidate for the presidential nomination, cast his tent in the South and camped there. After he received the nomination, he again camped in the South. And after his triumphant election he went back to the South to camp again. And it is only fair to say that no people can be more hospitable than southerners; and it may be added that none know better how to use hospitality to advance their plans and purposes. In the history of our republic, northern public men have repeatedly been wrecked on the shoals of southern hospitality. Mr. Taft had the opportunity and did study conditions at first hand. What are his conclusions?

In that portion of his inaugural address, his first state paper, in which he refers to southern conditions and the Negro people, he exposes, unwittingly to be sure, the hollow pretense and naked sham of all the prattle about the obliteration of section lines.

Mr. Taft refers to the South as a distinct section; he refers to the southern people as a distinct people; he laments the deplorable and menacing conditions existing in the South; and he makes a plaintive appeal for just laws, for due respect for the Constitution of the United States, for humane treatment of the Negro people and for recognition of their citizenship. To quote his words, he says: "I look forward with hope to increasing the already good feeling between the South and the other sections of the country. I look forward to an increase in the tolerance of political views of all kinds and their advocacy throughout the South. . . to an increased feeling on the part of all the people of the South that this government is their government and that its officers in their states are their officers. . . The Fifteenth Amendment has not been generally observed in the past, it ought to be observed. . . It never will be repealed, and it never ought to be repealed. The Negroes are now Americans—and this is their only country and their only flag. They have shown themselves anxious to live for it and die for it."

After this deliverance, Mr. Taft bent his knees to the Baal of southern race hate and race prejudice by declaring that he would not, or may not, appoint colored men to Federal offices if the white of the community should protest against it. This is a burlesque on Republican institutions. White men and colored men voted for the nomination of Mr. Taft; white men and colored men supported his candidacy and voted for his election. And white men and colored men—other things being equal—should share in the immunities and privileges under the government. The peace, prosperity and safety of this Republic demand that it shall be governed by law and justice, and not by race hate and race prejudice. Equal right for all the people is the only safety of all the people.

Address of

Rev. C. E. Stowe

I regret that it was known that I was in the room, but of course the interest is not in me or in my own personality, but in that of my mother, and that is the way I receive your tribute. I stand here simply to speak for her. Now with those self-effacing remarks, which are equally sincere, I wish to say that I am very glad to stand here as speaking for her and for her wonderful great love for all God's creatures. For I want to tell you from conviction, from observation, that the great power of Harriet Beecher Stowe and Henry Ward Beecher was not an intellectual power, but a marvellous power of loving. There have been men of greater genius than Henry Ward Beecher in many ways, but he was wonderful in his power of love and that was also the case with my own mother.

The writing of Uncle Tom's Cabin was the most remarkable thing in the world. Mrs. Stowe came to Boston in 1850, and stayed with her brother Edward at the Park Street church. I was only a baby at the time, and she had six little children with her. My Uncle Edward's wife said to my mother, "If I could write as you do, I would write something to make people feel what a curse, what an awful thing American slavery is." My sister, who was living at that time, told me she remembered it very well, although she was only a little girl thirteen years of age. She told me she remembered looking up into my mother's face, and she heard my

mother say "Isabella, I will if God gives me strength."
My father was a helpless invalid at that time. His
health broke down in Cincinnati in the Lane Theological
Seminary, he was not able to be of any assistance to them
in the seminary, and this little woman had to use her
right hand to earn money to move her family to Brunswick, Maine, where Professor Stowe had accepted a
professorship. She had a little baby at the time (I am
the result) and she wrote a letter afterwards to my
Uncle Edward's wife, Isabella, "I can't write anything
on that subject or anything else while I have to sleep
with the baby; but I will write it some time, God helping
me." I will say that I rather reluctantly confess that I
was a hindrance rather than a help to the book.

One afternoon as she was sitting in a little church in
Brunswick—she had no conception whatever of how to
develop any book—she was sitting in that little church
in Brunswick, and she said as she sat there, suddenly
without anything to indicate that such a psychological
phenomena was passing through her mind, she saw the
whole scene of the death of Uncle Tom pass before her
like a series of pictures. It seemed like the unrolling of
a panorama. She saw that terrible scene where Legre
threatens Uncle Tom. She saw him standing before
Legree; she saw the whole thing, picture after picture.
She broke into uncontrollable sobbing, and what came
to her with that series of pictures was "Inasmuch as ye
did it unto the least of one of these, ye did it unto me."
She saw Christ; and a voice said to her "Cry." She
went home—her husband was away—and she wrote out
what had passed before her in this vision. Her husband
being away, she gathered her little children around her,
three little girls and two little boys—of course I was
the infant, utterly unconscious of what was passing.
She began to read. The children all burst into sobbing,
and the little boy said, "Mamma, I can't hear it, slavery

is the most accursed thing on the face of this earth."
Friends, what happened in that family, happened all
over the country. I will not take advantage of the privilege given me to speak of it, but you must know how
near it is in my heart. I am glad to say that I recognize
thoroughly your appreciation of my mother, and for my
mother I receive it. She is not able to stand here before
you, so I simply stand here for her.

Address of

Rev. E. W. Moore

of

Philadelphia

The right of every American citizen to select his own society and invite whom he will to his parlor and table should be sacredly respected. A man's house is his castle, and he has the right to admit, or refuse admission, as he pleases. This right belongs to the humblest and the highest. The exercise of it by any of our citizens toward any body or class who may presume to intrude, should cause no complaint, for each and all may exercise the same right toward whom he will.

When he quits his home and goes upon the public street, enters a public car, or public house, he has no exclusive right of occupancy. He is only a part of the great public, and while he has the right to walk, ride and be accommodated with food and shelter in a public conveyance or hotel, he has no exclusive right to say that another citizen, tall or short, black or white, shall not be accorded the same civil treatment.

The argument against equality at hotels is very improperly put upon the ground that the exercise of such rights is social equality—but this ground is unreasonable. It is hard to say what social equality is, but it is certain that going into the same street car, hotel, or steamboat cabin does not make any man society for another, any more than flying in the air makes all birds of one feather.

The distinction between the two sorts of equality is broad and plain to the understanding of the most limited and yet, blinded by prejudice, men never cease to confound one with the other, and allow themselves to infringe the civil rights of their fellow-men as if those rights were, in some way, in violation of their social rights.

That this denial of rights to us is based on our race only as race is a badge of condition, is manifest in the fact that no matter how decently dressed or well-behaved a colored man may be, he is denied civil treatment in the ways thus pointed out, unless he comes as servant. His race, not his character, determines the place he shall hold and the kind of treatment he shall receive. That this is due to a prejudice that has no rational principle under it is seen in the fact that the presence of colored persons in hotels and railroad cars is only offensive when they are there as guests and passengers. As servants they are welcome, but as equal citizens they are not.

It is also seen in the fact that nowhere' else on the globe, except in the United States are colored people subjected to insult and outrage on account of race. The colored traveller in Europe does not meet with it, and we denounce it here as a disgrace to American civilization and American religion and as violation of the spirit and letter of the Constitution of the Unitea States.

From those courts which have solemnly sworn to support the Constitution and that yet treat this provision of it with contempt we appeal to the people, and call upon our friends to remember our civil rights at the ballot box. On the point of the two equalities we are determined to be understood.

We leave the social equality where it should be left, with each individual man and woman. No law can regulate or control it. It is a matter in which governments have nothing whatever to do. Each may choose his own friends and associates without interference or dictation of any.

Terrible as have been the outrages committed upon us in respect to our civil rights, more shocking and scandalous still have been the outrages committed upon our political rights which began by means of bull-dozing, ku-kluking, fraudulent counts, tissue ballots and like devices, until in many of the southern states they have set aside the Constitution of the United States. This has been done in face of the Republican party and under successive Republican administrations, So far as we are concerned, there is no government or Constitution of the United States.

To my mind, this is no question of party. It is a question of law and government. It is a question whether the government or the mob shall rule the land; whether the promises solemnly made to us in the Constitution be manfully kept or flagrantly broken.

Address of

Charles Edward Russell

Do I raise myself in any way by depressing my fellow man? Believe me, the idea contained in that suggestion is the heart and soul and substance of all there is in this race problem. There is no race problem, absolutely no race problem. The only problem is the problem of snobbery. The only thing that is involved in the position of the colored man in the South or in the North either, is a pure question of caste. That is all. Believe me, you are not discriminated against because your skins are dark, the color of your skin makes absolutely no difference. It is not involved in the matter at all.

Let me show you: A little while ago I was at the dinner table of a rich man of New York, eminent in society, and one of the guests was a man whose skin was much darker than the skins of most of you. He sat at that dinner table, the honored and petted guest, with more attention was paid to him than to anything else. His skin was dark, but the color of his skin had nothing to do with it. It is not because your skins are darker than ours, but because you are closer to nature, and the substance of caste and the substance of snobbery has been from the beginning that hatred of the man that works with his hands. It is not merely the idea of labor, but the idea of the lowest form of labor, which is slavery; it is the taint of slavery about you that makes you hateful to the snobbish man and nothing else. Low labor has always been detestable to the snobbish organization, and the most detestable of all labor, is the unpaid labor, the labor that is stolen. It is because you represent the unthinking man, that you are discriminated against.

I would like to issue a word of warning to two classes of my white fellow citizens, as to just exactly what this thing means that they have done to you. They have nullified two articles of the Constitution in order to get at you. I would like to tell two classes of my white fellow men what that means. First to the white working man: They have nullified that part of the Constitution that guarantees the franchise, irrespective of color. That has been done at the demand of a dominant class. Under conceivable conditions it would be just exactly as feasible, just as easy, to deprive the white working man of the franchise, as it has been to deprive the colored man. The next warning is that if they can nullify the Constitution with regard to franchise, they can nullify it with regard to anything else. Look out! Look out! Under conceivable circumstances it will be just exactly as easy to nullify that clause of the Constitution which guarantees property against confiscation without due process of law—just as easy. Because, as a matter of fact, if there is any part of the constitution that is not valid, there is no part of it that is valid. If there is one thing in that Constitution that cannot be enforced, there is nothing in it that can be enforced.

RESOLUTIONS

The Conference, after considerable discussion, then adopted the following resolutions:

"We denounce the ever-growing oppression of our 10,000,000 colored fellow citizens as the greatest menace that threatens the country. Often plundered of their just share of the public funds, robbed of nearly all part in the government, segregated by common carriers,* some murdered with impunity, and all treated with open contempt by officials, they are held in some States in practical slavery to the white community. The systematic persecution of law-abiding citizens and their disfranchisement on account of their race alone is a crime that will ultimately drag down to an infamous end any nation that allows it to be practised, and it bears most heavily on those poor white farmers and laborers whose economic position is most similar to that of the persecuted race."

"The nearest hope lies in the immediate and patiently continued enlightenment of the people who have been inveigled into a campaign of oppression. The spoils of persecution should not go to enrich any class or classes of the population. Indeed persecution of organized workers, peonage, enslavement of prisoners, and even disfranchisement already threaten large bodies of whites in many Southern States."

*The insertion of the phrase "segregated by common carriers" was moved as an amendment by Mr. William M. Trotter.

"We agree fully with the prevailing opinion that the transformation of the unskilled colored laborers in industry and agriculture into skilled workers is of vital importance* to that race and to the nation, but we demand for the Negroes, as for all others, a free and complete education, whether by city, State, or nation, a grammar school and industrial training for all, and technical, professional, and academic education for the most gifted."

"But the public schools assigned to the Negro of whatever kind or grade will never receive a fair and equal treatment until he is given equal treatment in the Legislature and before the law. Nor will the practically educated Negro, no matter how valuable to the community he may prove, be given a fair return for his labor or encouraged to put forth his best efforts or given the chance to develop that efficiency that comes only outside the school until he is respected in his legal rights as a man and a citizen."

"We regard with grave concern the attempt manifest South and North to deny to black men the right to work and to enforce this demand by violence and bloodshed. Such a question is too fundamental and clear even to be submitted to arbitration. The late strike in Georgia is not simply a demand that Negroes be displaced, but that proven and efficient men be made to surrender their long followed means of livelihood to white competitors."

"As first and immediate steps toward remedying

*The phrase originally read "of great importance to that race." Mr. Ransome moved as an amendment that it be altered to "of first importance." Bishop Walters moved as an amendment to the amendment that the words should read "of vital importance." This amendment was **carried**. Mr. Ransome's amendment was then unanimously **carried**.

223

these national wrongs, so full of peril for the whites as well as the blacks of all sections, we demand* of Congress and the Executive:

(1.) That the Constitution be strictly enforced and the civil rights guaranteed under the Fourteenth Amendment be secured impartially to all.

(2.) That there be equal educational opportunities for all and in all the States, and that public school expenditure be the same for the Negro and white child.

(3.) That in accordance with the Fifteenth Amendment the right of the Negro to the ballot on the same terms as other citizens be recognized in every part of the country."

The committee on permanent organization in its report proposed a resolution providing for "the incorporation of a national committee to be known as a Committee for the Advancement of the Negro Race, to aid their progress and make their citizenship a reality, with all the rights and privileges pertaining thereto." It presented also a resolution calling for a committee of forty charged with the organization of a national committee with power to call the convention in 1910.

The resolution proposed by Mr. Trotter was referred to the committee on resolutions and was reported back and adopted in the following form:

"We deplore any recognition of, or concession to, prejudice or color by the federal government in any officer or branch thereof, as well as the presidential declaration on the appointment of colored men to office in the South, contradicting as it does the President's just and admirable utterance against the pro-

*The words "we demanded" were inserted on the motion of Mr. Greener. This amendment was unanimously carried.

posed disfranchisement of the colored voters of Maryland.

Mr. Trotter proposed a resolution demanding that lynching be made a federal crime. The resolution was referred to the committee on resolutions which reported that it held the question of lynching to be covered in the main resolution by the words "murdered with impunity." Mr. Trotter's resolution was lost by a vote of fifty-three to twenty-one.

The following Committee of Forty was then named: William English Walling, chairman, New York; Rev. W. H. Brooks, New York; Prof. John Dewey, New York; Paul Kennedy, New York; Jacob W. Mack, New York; Mrs. Mary MacLean, New York; Dr. Henry Moskowitz, New York; John E. Milholland, New York; Miss Leonora O'Reilly, New York; Charles Edward Russell, New York; Prof. Edwin R. A. Seligman, New York; Oswald G. Villard, New York; Miss Lillian D. Wald, New York; Bishop Alexander Walters, New York; Dr. Stephen S. Wise, New York; Miss Mary W. Ovington, Brooklyn, N. Y.; Dr. O. M. Waller, Brooklyn, N. Y.; Rev. J. H. Holmes, Yonkers, N. Y.; Prof. W. L. Bulkley, Ridgefield Park, N. J.; Miss Maria Baldwin, Boston, Mass.; Archibald H. Grimké, Boston, Mass.; Albert E. Pillsbury, Boston, Mass.; Moorfield Storey, Boston, Mass.; Pres. Chas. P. Thwing, Cleveland, O.; Pres. W. S. Scarborough, Wilberforce, O.; Miss Jane Addams, Chicago, Ill.; Mrs. Ida Wells Barnett, Chicago, Ill.; Dr. C. E. Bentley, Chicago, Ill.; Mrs. Celia Parker Woolley, Chicago, Ill.; Dr. William Sinclair, Philadelphia, Pa.; Miss Susan Wharton, Philadelphia, Pa.; R. R. Wright, Jr., Philadelphia, Pa.; L. M. Hershaw, Washington, D. C.; Judge Wendell P. Stafford, Washington, D. C.; Mrs. Mary Church Terrell, Washington, D. C.; Rev. J. Milton Waldron, Washington, D. C.; Prof. W. E. B. DuBois, Atlanta, Ga.; Leslie Pinckney Hill, Manassas, Va.

LETTER FROM MR. WILLIAM LLOYD
GARRISON, BOSTON

I regret my inability to be present at the Conference and record my protest against the rising tide of race prejudice and caste. Every step in that direction needs to be unflinchingly met, regardless of the eminent respectability that now lends countenance to this resurgent spirit of slavery. As in former days, the most insidious betrayal of freedom comes from its professed friends.

The Vardamans and Tillmans are harmless in comparison. Their brutal avowal of a purpose to reduce the Negro to a state of permanent vassalage, through evasion or defiance of the Constitution and law, repels humane souls and makes for justice. It is men of so-called light and leading, solicitous regarding social problems, arrogating to themselves the character of friendly advisers of the colored people, yet viewing the question from the summit of race pride and birth, who are most to be feared.

From these come easy acquiescence in the abrogation of the Fifteenth Amendment, the approval of separate schools based on complexion, and an affected horror of racial intermarriage for fear of white deterioration—while contemplating without disturbance the unabated illicit connections so flagrantly in evidence. The creed leads to servitude, in another form, of the people liberated by Lincoln's proclamation; compassing by force or fraud the end for which the Southern Confederacy fought and failed. Now, as then, democracy is in the balance The issue will determine whether self-government can survive in a land where material interests long overshadow the principles and enthusiasms of liberty. It is the fair-weather soothsayers who drug the public conscience and weaken resistance to privilege.

I trust that the Conference will utter no uncertain sound on any point affecting the vital subject. No part of it is too delicate for plain speech. The republican experiment is at stake, every tolerated wrong to the Negro reacting with double force upon white citizens guilty of faithlessness to their brothers. The rampant antipathy to the Oriental races is part and parcel of the domestic question. Safety lies in an absolute refusal to differentiate the rights of human beings. Each has equal claim to life, liberty, and the pursuit of happiness, no outworn formula, in spite of the fashion of the mighty to deride it.

I put political rights before educational. Universities have no difficulty in rearing despots, and the wicked laws of all nations are the handiwork of men taught in the schools. Let ignorance, blunder, and bad laws result. Under impartial self-government the blunderers reap the punishment and learn wisdom and self-restraint. No college compares with this primary school of civilization in educating a people. Learning never yet guaranteed rights; rights universally secured are the sure guaranty of learning. Let the unanimous voice of the Conference be lifted for justice and opportunity to all races, colors, and sexes without distinction, in face of the casuistry all abounding in this darkened day.

Yours, for a united humanity,

WM. LLOYD GARRISON.

LETTER FROM MR. BRAND WHITLOCK
MAYOR OF TOLEDO, OHIO

No one who loves the ideals of America and believes fundamentally in democracy, in the equality and brotherhood of men, as I do, can regard the present temper of a large portion of our people toward the Negro with any emotion other than sadness.

The problem which this condition presents is profound and difficult, and the solution will demand our best thought and most enlightened sympathies. The nation went through a dreadful war to give the Negro political freedom, and yet even that has not been accomplished, except in a formal, legal sense; and even in that department there are so many proposals and even achievements in retrogression, that to-day the Negro is ostracized and by many proscribed and hated. The question is no longer what we once considered it, namely, a sectional one; it has become a national one. The Negro is treated as contemptuously and used as hardly in the North as in the South. There is even arising among us a kind of snobbery, the most detestable that can be imagined—namely, an affected dislike of the Negro, considered as an evidence of superiority and aristocracy.

The problem is not only social or political; it has its economic side, and more mysterious and baffling than any of these, its psychological and ethnic side. It must be studied in all these various phases. Many profound and learned articles have been written by the eminent and the learned, in which it is insisted that we study the Negro. But it seems to me that we need quite as much to study ourselves. The white race has been two centuries in creating this problem, and according to the law of moral action and reaction, the law of moral equivalents and balances, we cannot in forty-five years solve a problem which we were two hundred years in creating. I do not think the problem is insoluble; I do not think any problem is insoluble, and I think we shall solve this problem only as we recognize and believe devoutly in the ideals and principles of America, which, if they mean anything at all, mean that all men without distinction, are to be free and equal, at least, in opportunity. That is what America is for, and the true American spirit cannot exist until America is for all men on equal terms, no matter who or what they are, or who or what they were, or where they came from, or what they believe, or what their race or color. We can solve this problem, we can solve any problem in politics and economics properly only by adhering to these fundamental principles of our America, only by keeping in mind that truth so well expressed by Mr. Howells:

"The first thing you have to learn here below is that in essentials you are just like everyone else, and that you are different from others only in what is not so much worth while. If you have anything in common with your fellow-creatures, it is something that God gave you; if you have anything that seems quite your own, it is from your silly self, and is a sort of perversion of what came to you from the Creator who made you out of himself, and had nothing else to make any one out of. There is not really any difference between you and your fellow-creatures; but only a seeming difference that flatters and cheats you with a sense of your strangeness and makes you think you are a remarkable fellow."